THE
PLANT LOVER'S GUIDE
TO
PRIMULAS

THE **PLANT LOVER'S GUIDE** TO
PRIMULAS

JODIE MITCHELL & LYNNE LAWSON

TIMBER PRESS
PORTLAND, OREGON

CONTENTS

61

100 Primulas for the Garden

189

Growing and Propagating

WHY WE LOVE PRIMULAS

Primula vulgaris has a magical quality about it.

Just yellow flowers in the hedgerows or garish pot plants in supermarkets? Until 20 odd years ago that is all primroses meant to me, but then my husband and I moved to France, by chance just a mile away from the newly relocated Barnhaven Primroses nursery. I began working there as a pollinator and a whole new world was opened up. The wild primrose remains one of my favourites, but oh, there are so many more. I never would have believed that primroses are a tiny part of a vast genus that has more than 430 species, ranging from the tiniest rock plant to majestic candelabras.

Primroses are very modest plants; they don't (apart from a few species like *Primula vialii*) shout out "look at me," but they do go about their business beautifying the world quietly. They are very natural looking flowers, with nothing artificial about them, apart from perhaps some of the spectacular Show auriculas. They are the very essence and freshness of spring and bring with them the hope of a new year and new beginnings.

Probably the most important aspect of this group to me is colour, and that's usually the first thing visitors remark on when they enter our nursery. Almost every colour of the

An unnamed double primrose, one of the latest results from Lynne's double breeding programme.

spectrum can be found in primulas and it is possible to have endless matching shades and nuances from pale China silk to the darkest navy, from shell pinks to rose and geranium, from frosty whites, chamois, rich yellows to tawny nasturtium shades, from new and resonant reds to profoundly deep velvet ones.

I love their endless variation. We grow our plants from seed obtained by hand pollination. This means that each plant is unique and different from its companions in terms of colour shade and form. When selecting for breeding, we could choose the plants to be as uniform as possible in each series, but we prefer to reflect nature's abundant variation in the number of shades and forms that we allow to be included. Breeding primulas is the most fascinating part of my work. The plants have a great willingness to change form and colour according to our aspirations, though admittedly also a dogged determination to hold onto an undesired trait bred in by mistake.

I love their versatility and adaptability. There are primulas to fit most gardens and conditions from damp and shady to warm and dry. Most *Primula* species are not too fussy, and given some shade and some reasonable earth to grow in, they'll reward you by flowering away and will return season after season. I love the way you can use them to suit your own tastes, either in formal or natural planting. In the garden, they can be star players or have a supporting role to show off other plants. They can be planted in a mass to make a statement or dotted about to complement shrubs or other plants. There are varieties for everybody, from the easy to, shall we say, the more challenging.

All primulas do well in pots—you just have to suit the container to the variety. Candelabras, for instance, have very deep roots, so to do well they need a really big container, whereas a tiny marginata will eventually fill a small shallow dish and be so smothered in flowers that you can't see the leaves.

Last, but not least, I love their scent. Yes, it's subtle and needs a little warmth to draw it out, but what can beat the first sniff of the first wild primrose posy of the season to lift your spirits on a cold day in early spring?

— **Lynne Lawson**

The first primroses I remember seeing were the yellow primroses dotted about the Breton lanes and hedgerows. They are for me synonymous with my discovery of the countryside as a child. Having moved from the outskirts of suburban Manchester in the north of England, I was suddenly free to roam about the woods, making bouquets of wild flowers, listening to the bird song, and looking for mice and snakes. Wild *Primula vulgaris* is still one of my favourites because, as for many people, it has that association with a certain forgotten youth or bygone era. The flowers have a magical glow especially at dusk and in the early morning light.

As a young girl, the first primrose I grew was polyanthus 'Daybreak', gifted to me by Angela Bradford, the previous owner of Barnhaven who happened to live a short bike ride away in the same village. I cleared away a patch in the nettles and brambles in the back garden of the old French café my family had moved into and there my primrose flowered away nearly all year. With my parents, I started helping out in the nursery, graduating from cleaning plants to helping with the pollinating. Some of my most vivid memories are of the sweet, almost sickly smell of the Border auriculas that stick to your fingers, the sound of bees buzzing drowsily in early summer, collecting the stamps that came from all over the world with the seed orders, and hearing the bell ringing for tea.

Then I went away to study and started having my own gardens. Wherever I went, a few primroses would come with me, a particular favourite remaining the drumstick primula (*Primula denticulata*) with its globe-headed flowers. In places where I didn't have a garden, I would make do with a few pots of juliana primroses. Then I started visiting gardens in the United Kingdom and elsewhere and discovered the breathtaking displays of mass plantings of candelabra primroses, the huge variety of alpine primulas, and the never-ending supply of species and cultivars that makes *Primula*, in my eyes, the most fascinating genus.

When I came to join my parents after they had taken over the nursery, I delved more into the history and background of many of the plants we grew and my interest grew even deeper from there. From the story of the Show auriculas that spans centuries, to the brave plant hunters of the eighteenth century that brought many of the Asiatic species to Europe, to the still relatively undocumented history of *Primula sieboldii* cultivars or the origins of the modern polyanthus, there is so much more to many of these unassuming modest plants than meets the eye.

Aside from the history of the plants, it is also great to realize that there is a type of primula for nearly every type of garden or should I say every type of gardener. There is a primrose for the novice gardener who is simply looking for an easy reliable plant to brighten up their front windowsill, for the ambitious gardener with grand ideas of mass planting, to the experienced botanist who is looking for rare species that no one else has got, for the competitive grower who wants to grow the best auriculas to show, for the average urban gardener looking for some spring colour for a difficult shady patch. Primulas are such versatile plants, and we hope that with this book we can entice more people to grow more of this fascinating and not always widely known genus.

—Jodie Mitchell

The Barnhaven Story—Something of a Fairy Tale

Florence Bellis

The barn at Barnhaven.

In the Great Depression of the 1930s in Oregon, a young concert pianist called Florence Bellis was out of work, ill, and destitute. She found refuge, with her two pianos and husband, in an old barn, without running water or electricity but surrounded by a wonderful creek area and an old apple orchard with good, rich soil. It was a haven for Florence—hence the name Barnhaven.

As well as the pianos, she had brought with her some trays of seedling primroses. In a friend's English catalogue she had seen some pictures of primroses and had fallen in love with them. With her last five dollars, as the story goes, she had ordered several packets of Suttons polyanthus seed from England. At the time she had never read a garden book, never even grown a plant, but she did have a "naïve, absolute confidence" and went on to embark on a hybridizing programme that transformed the primula world and made horticultural history.

At that time there was a very limited colour range in polyanthus. Florence's first list in 1939 offered just scarlet, crimson, orange, yellow, and white (and she forgot to include the prices). She was an instinctive plant breeder, obsessed by colour, and she went on to introduce the first true blues and pinks, which caused a sensation, and literally hundreds of other identifiable colour shades. She concentrated too on fragrance and form and described Barnhaven's hallmark as "a triad of colour, lilting grace, with overtones of fragrance."

She was the first to hand-pollinate primroses commercially, and that practice is continued at Barnhaven today. She had no idea how to do it, so simply started by taking the flowers apart and applying pollen directly to the stigmas, no brushes, sterilizing, bagging involved. She worked extensively on anomalous primroses, auriculas, Gold-laced polyanthus, julianas, and her famous double primroses.

Florence grew upward of 200,000 plants per year, not in tiny plugs in tunnels as we see today, but planted out in the open, and her customers, who came from far and wide, chose their plants by putting sticks next to specimens they wanted in the orchard. Florence went on to form the American Primrose Society in 1947 and was a prolific contributor to many journals and newspapers.

When the time came to retire in 1966 she refused to sell her valuable seed strains to the large seed houses and instead chose to send a sample of all of them to the Sinclairs, customers of hers, in the Lake District in northwestern England with the message "yours to keep or kill." Fortunately for all of us, the Sinclairs decided to "keep" and thus the Barnhaven story continued in England for another 20 years or more. Florence's work was not only continued but was also extensively enhanced and improved. The Sinclairs added another 11 new strains and worked tirelessly on *Primula sieboldii* and double primroses.

In 1990 Barnhaven moved to France under the care of Angela Bradford. Again, seed samples were passed on, and against all odds the work was continued until 2000 when David and Lynne Lawson took up the mantle, somewhat with trepidation because of the responsibility of continuing such a legend. The future of Barnhaven is in safe hands as their daughter Jodie and family have joined the ranks and have brought new life, energy, and ideas, and most of all, the necessary passion and dedication to continue this painstaking work.

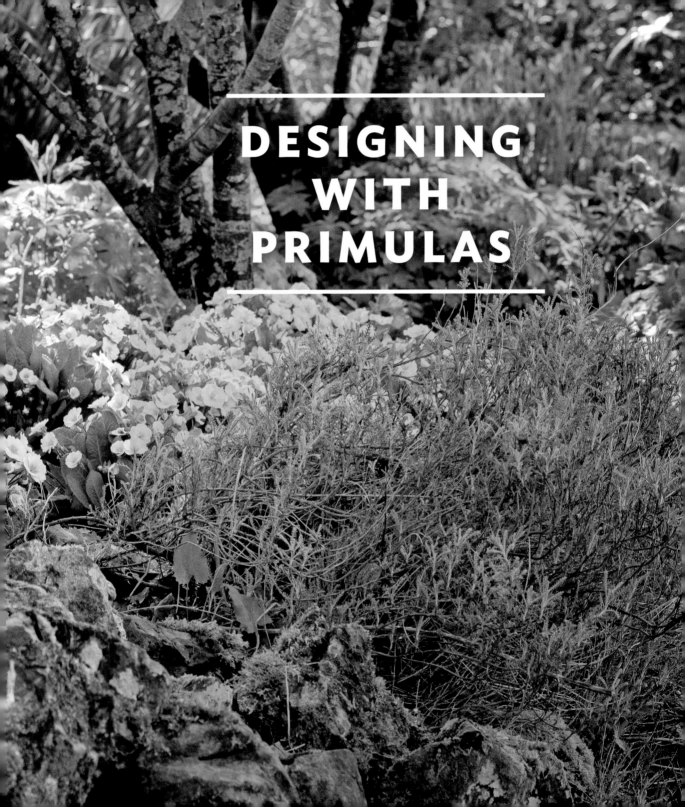

DESIGNING WITH PRIMULAS

The gentle colours of yellow and pink acaulis primroses combine readily.

H

Historically, and it's often the case today, primulas have been used as annual spring bedding, planted in formal beds and discarded at the end of the season, which is why many people still consider them as nonhardy, somewhat garish bedding plants. Of course, they can be used as a simple way of adding a bright splash of spring colour to formal beds or to a window box; however, this is a very limited use of a large genus of very hardy perennial plants.

When primroses are planted in the right place with sufficient shade in the summer and enough moisture, you will be able to enjoy a large range of flowering forms year after year in nearly every kind of garden, be it big or small. We have focused here on a selection of easy-to-grow garden plants that are extremely hardy and can be grown with relatively little fuss. We could only include a very small snapshot of this vast horticultural group, but hope that we will encourage you to try a few in your own garden and to see what else is out there.

What Primulas Contribute to the Garden

There are many uses for primulas and here are some of the main reasons why every garden should have some.

COLOUR

Primulas can be found in nearly all colours of the spectrum, which is why they are such a versatile plant if you are looking for a specific colour theme. Not only that, but when planted with other primulas, they rarely clash and will combine harmoniously with many other plants. They usually have gentle colours that can blend together with a beauty that only nature can provide in soft hues of pinks, yellows, and blues. Some of them can be very striking. A large drift of the candelabra *Primula pulverulenta* and its bright pink flowers makes a very bold statement whereas few gardeners can resist the charm of the palest of moonlight yellows of the common European primrose (*P. vulgaris*).

Primroses can provide a riot of welcome colour in early spring.

Apart from the choice of colours, primroses make a vital contribution in the garden as there is so little other colour in the first months of the year. Maybe they would be overlooked in the vibrant summer months, but the first appearance of the bright colours of the early primroses through melting snow or the drab earth is a delight to the senses.

FLOWERING PERIOD

Contrary to popular belief, you can have primula in flower for many more months of the year than just two or three months in early spring. Growing different varieties together, such as some of the juliana hybrids with some of the later-flowering cowslips, can greatly extend the early display. When winter is mild, many polyanthus and primroses appear even in late autumn and can continue flowering until late spring. Many Asiatic primulas, such as *Primula grandis*, *P. involucrata*, and *P. parryi* from the high mountain meadows of the Himalayas, begin to flower as the early primroses finish, with the fairylike blossoms of *P. sieboldii* and of course the vast candelabra group. Others flower even later in early summer and midsummer, such as *P. alpicola* and *P. vialii*, and for a glorious finale, *P. florindae* with its stately perfumed bells flowering until late summer, often joined by *P. capitata* for a generous second flowering of the year.

One of the earliest flowers of the year, *Primula denticulata* often appears when the snow melts.

Primula vialii, also called orchid primrose, is one of the most unusual-looking primroses.

Among the smallest forms are rock-hugging alpines such as *Primula* 'Gloria Johnstone' shown here.

VARIETY OF SIZE AND FORM

There is incredible variety in the primula family. How many times have we heard people walking round our nursery asking "Is this a primrose too?" or saying "This can't be a primrose!" Not only do the flowers vary enormously from the tiniest of blossoms to generous multipetalled doubles, from flat open flowers to bell shapes, globes, or even spears, but plant size also varies hugely from tiny rock garden plants such as *P. marginata*, which is only 6 inches (15 cm) high, to the statuesque candelabras that can grow up to 3 feet (1 metre) tall.

The foliage also varies greatly. Some forms of *Primula denticulata* have huge cabbagelike leaves after flowering which can help stop the spread of weeds, whereas some of the smaller alpines have very interesting spiky, powdery leaves that need to be admired up close. This variation can create continuous interest in the garden and gives the gardener a huge choice of different styles of plants.

PLANTS FOR A VARIETY OF CULTURAL CONDITIONS

Because primulas come from such varying parts of the world, there are plants for a wide range of garden conditions. In the wild, they grow in woodland, grassy banks, wet mountainous meadows and high alpine pastures, on banks of streams, and rocky outcrops. They are generally native to the Northern Hemisphere. This explains why they typically prefer cool and damp climates though they will adapt to warmer places if given the right conditions. We know several people who grow primroses successfully in Australia, Alaska, and northern Norway.

Most primulas are suitable for the average garden. They are not terribly fussy plants, and given a modicum of shade and average well-drained soil, they should thrive even in frost pockets and difficult shady areas. Even if you feel your garden is too hot and dry for primulas to be at home, you can still put some plants in pots and place them by a shady front door for a warm welcome where you can keep an eye on the watering.

PLANTS FOR EVERY TYPE AND SIZE OF GARDEN

There are primroses for nearly every kind of garden or landscape design. For the average urban gardener who has lots of shade, a few primroses can brighten up a dark corner, and a couple of strategically placed containers on the terrace can be enjoyed from the house while it is still too cold to venture out. Even where there is no garden, a small north-facing balcony or windowsill will easily accommodate a small collection of auriculas. The

Caher Bridge Garden, a private garden in Ireland, has a large collection of well-grown primulas.

other advantage of them being relatively small plants is that you don't need much space to amass a large collection. But beware! They are addictive.

Like most smaller spring flowers, primulas make a greater impact planted in groups. In a large garden, a few primroses here and there will get lost, but a drift of self-seeding candelabras or belled primulas down by a stream can make a huge impact and a mass of *Primula sieboldii* meandering away under trees can turn any area into a fairy dell. There are many types of primulas that are a lot more difficult to grow and are best confined to an alpine house or cold greenhouse, but in this book we have chosen only the more garden friendly species that have proved their worth.

PLANTS FOR A VARIETY OF GARDEN SITUATIONS

If you want to get the best out of your primroses, their location in the garden is, as for most plants, of utmost importance. If they are planted in a dry, sunny place, they will dwindle away in a couple of years, and if the site is really hot are unlikely to make it through their first summer. If you plant an auricula in a waterlogged garden on heavy soil, it is likely not to survive the winter. As there are so many types of primulas there isn't a one-site-fits-all, but the basic rules of summer shade, moisture, and fairly rich soil apply to all the groups.

A huge variety of garden situations will suit primroses. The best way to choose where to plant your primulas is to try and replicate as near as possible the growing conditions in the wild. Whereas most of us don't have a 3000-foot (900-metre) mountain in the garden, with a bit of imagination we can replicate a cliff face with a small rockery, a stream with a moist area in the garden with perhaps an overflow from a barrel collecting rainwater, and a woodland by planting them under herbaceous shrubs. What is great about primulas is that if you feel they are not doing well where you have planted them—for example, they are not bulking up and thriving—it is very easy to move them as they are pretty amenable to transplanting. Sometimes it is just a matter of moving them a few metres away to a spot that provides them with a bit more shade or less competition.

We are often asked if it is possible to naturalize hybrid primulas in a lawn as is done in many areas of France where native primroses self-seed all over the place, are mown regularly, and come back the following spring. We don't recommend deliberately naturalizing hybrids in a lawn, especially one that is beautifully manicured, as the primrose roots will struggle to compete with the dense grass and the compacted soil. Much better to plant primulas in a shady border and see what other colours come up in the lawn when the bees have done their work.

ATTRACTIVE TO INSECTS

Primulas are a great pollen provider for bees and other insects, especially in early spring when few other plants are in bloom. There is no need here to emphasize the importance of looking out for these vital insects, and even in a small garden you can do your bit.

SCENT

In our opinion, primroses should smell . . . and very few in the wild don't. Most of the varieties we have included in this book are sweetly scented. The scent is usually quite subtle but so very welcome as soon as the sun comes out and you catch the first wafts. If scent is a big must for you, the most scented primulas are the belled varieties such as *Primula alpicola* and *P. florindae*. Another unforgettable one for scent is *P. munroi*.

LET THE FUN BEGIN

So you planted some white primroses in the garden and now there are some pink ones growing in a completely different place. Yes, this is normal and just means that the bees have been promiscuous with some of the red primroses growing next door. This happens frequently with *Primula* species. Generally, most species from the same group will cross, so for example, most of the candelabras will hybridize together, but you can't cross an auricula with a polyanthus. If primulas self-seed in your garden, you will have a stunning array of different colours. You may even find the odd double primrose or naturally occurring Jack-in-the-Green form. However, the mother plant will stay true to form year after year and you can propagate it easily by division.

Border auriculas make a stunning display in a well-drained border.

Candelabras at the Royal Horticultural Society's Garden Harlow Carr. Most of the candelabras will hybridize with each other, creating a riot of colour.

Polyanthus primulas are often used as colourful bedding plants.

Irish Kennedy primroses planted between steps at Blarney Castle in Ireland.

Design Ideas

Primulas can be grown in garden borders; in woodland and under trees; in rock gardens, rockeries, and crevices; and near streams and ponds. They also can be grown in pots.

IN THE BORDER

Nearly all primulas included in this book grow in the average garden border, including all the primroses, polyanthus, and *Primula sieboldii* hybrids. Candelabras and many of the Asiatic species will also look stunning as long as they get enough water in summer months, and the Border auriculas are ideal if they are in a well-drained position.

Most primroses and polyanthus will work in informal settings and formal bedding planting schemes. The most common primula used in formal bedding is the polyanthus, which comes in such a stunning array of colours. Why not be inspired by some of the planting in the local parks and public gardens?

Many colour combinations are suitable for formal gardens, but some of the nicest ones that we've seen use two contrasting colours such as pink polyanthus with white tulips or purple and orange polyanthus. Other primulas can also be used in a surprising formal way. One example is to plant *Primula florindae* in rows in front of tall grasses.

Border auriculas, as the name suggests, were often planted in the path leading up to the front door in

In spring the primroses make a lovely display.

The foliage of the herbaceous perennials creates shade in the summer months

Victorian gardens. This use is perfect if you have a very shady front garden, for example, where the plants will look stunning simply by themselves or planted under some traditional rose bushes that provide shade in the summer.

For more informal borders, primroses and polyanthus work wonderfully well grown in herbaceous beds. The primroses will be very visible at flowering time and then the other perennials such as peonies and grasses can take over, providing much-needed shade for the primroses. Even if you only have a very small space, two or three plants can brighten up a shady corner. We also recommend the juliana hybrids, which will spread fairly readily and form a small carpet of flowers, as well as the acaulis forms and polyanthus, although many of the other primulas would work very well too.

For a real cottagey look, the acaulis primroses and cowslips look lovely in more naturalistic planting schemes such as at the foot of a north-facing bank or dotted about at the edges of paths, where they will self-seed.

WOODLAND AND UNDER TREES

Plenty of primroses are well suited in a woodland type of situation as this is closest to their native habitat. *Primula sieboldii* hybrids and *P. kisoana* are two examples. These primroses spread readily in shady conditions to provide groundcover, but there are many others to choose from including all the primroses and polyanthus and many of the candelabras and belled primulas.

Those lucky enough to have a large garden with a small copse or woodland can easily provide a great environment of dappled shade. Primulas do especially well under deciduous trees, which gives them plenty of sun in early spring and shade later in summer when the tree leaves have grown. Such plants are at their best when a naturalized system of

Primula sieboldii Manakoora Group in a shady border.

mass planting is adopted rather than planting them in regimented rows. The candelabra primulas are well suited to these conditions as long as the soil is rich and damp enough. Most of the colours of *Primula japonica* forms work well together and are impressive in a large array of different shades.

You can extend the flowering season by including earlier flowering *Primula denticulata* in various shades and *P. vialii* for later blooms.

Traditionally, primroses were often grown in orchards where they would profit from the manure spread around the foot of the trees. Florence Bellis used to grow hers in the old orchard at the original Barnhaven gardens in Oregon. Circular beds round the foot of a small fruit tree in an urban garden can replicate this effectively and look striking when underplanted with one variety of polyanthus.

ROCK GARDENS, ROCKERIES, AND CREVICE GARDENS

No rockery or alpine garden is complete without its fair share of primulas. Many *Primula* species come from mountainous regions, such as the alpine primula and auriculas, and would do well in these well-drained situations. They tolerate more sun than many of the other primula groups, but bear in mind that they like cool roots and do not thrive in poor soil. They prefer a north- or east-facing section of the rockery if possible or to be tucked into specially made pockets of enriched soil under the shade of large rocks or shrubs. At the base of the rockery where the conditions are moister, you can grow other varieties such as the juliana hybrids or *P. capitata*, which will also appreciate the well-drained conditions.

Primula pulverulenta hybrids in a woodland setting in Fairhaven Woodland and Water Garden, Norfolk, England.

Pam Eveleigh's rock garden in Calgary, Canada, is a primula lover's delight.

Water feature and *Primula pulverulenta* in the rock garden at Cragside in Northumberland, England.

Crevice gardens are an alternative way of recreating the mountainous conditions that many of the smaller alpines enjoy tucked against rocky outcrops. On a smaller scale, you can recreate these conditions in a stone trough or pot with a few slates propped on their sides and some rocks. Many growers use hypertufa rocks and troughs, which are made from a cement, peat, and perlite mix. This mixture creates a light, well-draining, natural-looking stone that is easy to manipulate and is very effective. You can find plenty of information online on how to make these.

In a rock garden that features running water, belled primulas and candelabras, both natives of the high mountains of the Himalayas, are an obvious choice and blend in beautifully with this environment.

Primula marginata growing in a stone trough.

NEAR STREAMS AND PONDS

If you have a bog garden area, a stream or pond, or even just a damp area in your garden, nothing is better than the wide range of candelabra or belled primulas which are often classified as bog garden primulas. *Primula vialii*, *P. rosea*, and *P. denticulata* will also flourish in these conditions and help turn what can be a tricky patch into an area of outstanding beauty.

Nothing is more breathtaking than candelabras and other bog garden primulas planted en masse. Most will thrive at the edge of streams and ponds, in ground that is always moist but never completely waterlogged in winter. They also tolerate sunnier conditions than some of the other primulas do if their feet are kept damp. Here they form huge plants with big fleshy roots and self-seed readily. Most of the belled primulas are heavily perfumed.

One of the few primulas that tolerates being completely submerged is *Primula florindae*. It also is one of the latest to bloom, producing a mass of yellow flowers.

IN THE HOME

Although this book is only concerned with hardy primulas for the garden, there are several varieties that are grown for house plants, such as *Primula malacoides* and *P. obconica*, both of which are widely available from garden centres. (Be aware that some people are very allergic to the leaves.). Although the hardy garden plants are not happy for long periods indoors, it is possible to bring them into a cool room for up to two to three weeks (longer than a shop-bought bunch of flowers). Either dig up a plant growing in the garden when it is just in bud and pot it up, or keep some plants in pots that you have sown from seed and simply plant them in the garden after their time as a house decoration is over.

Primulas can also be used in flower arranging and are really useful for the vase when not much else is in flower. The polyanthus types with their long stems are a good choice as well as *Primula sieboldii*.

Good Planting Companions

While primulas can look great planted in large groups of contrasting or harmonious colours, it is worth putting a bit of thought into companion plants that will show them off to their full advantage. There are several considerations when choosing partners for your primulas. You can enrich the tapestry of colours with plants that flower at similar times or use foliage plants that will provide a great backdrop when they are in flower and create beneficial shade to help maintain the cool, moist soil that primulas thrive on. Depending on your climate or the exposure of your plants in the garden, this extra summer shade may even be essential to ensure that your primulas grow to their best advantage.

Most primulas flower for about three months, which means that unless you are prepared to dig them up every year and move them to a shady corner once they have finished flowering, you have to consider what other plants to use in that area to extend the interest over the year. This is especially true when using *Primula sieboldii* hybrids, which disappear completely in late summer.

There is a huge array of good companions for primulas and we cannot even skim the surface of all the possibilities. Whether you are planning a small container or a huge border, the main thing is to choose plants that will thrive in the same conditions enjoyed by the different groups.

Remember that not all primulas flower at the same time, so you can hugely extend the flowering season by planting different types of primulas. For example, to have flowers from late winter to early summer, you could plant some early flowering juliana hybrids with some of the late-flowering cowslips against a backdrop of *Primula japonica*.

TREES AND SHRUBS

The garden's structure is particularly evident in winter, and to do justice to the relatively small blooms of the early primroses it is worth thinking about creating a backdrop of evergreen shrubs and trees. Early spring flowering trees such as scented witch hazels, magnolias, amelanchiers, or camellias contribute much to the overall early spring display.

Primulas thrive under deciduous trees that allow the sunlight to filter through the branches and provide much-needed shade in summer, as long as the primulas are not planted too near the tree roots which can make the soil dry out too much. In a small garden, you can recreate a woodland effect with just one small tree such as *Prunus serrula* whose bark will be stunning in late winter and early spring and whose pink flowers will coincide with midspring flowering primulas.

Flowering currants like *Ribes sanguineum* are stunning in midspring with their frothy pink or white flowers underplanted with white or pink primroses. Another combination is *R. sanguineum* var. *glutinosum* 'White Icicle' with *Primula* Harvest Yellows Group.

Azealas and rhododendrons are perfect companions for the later-flowering primulas such as *Primula sieboldii* and the candelabras as they love the same acidic conditions. You will need to be careful when choosing rhododendrons especially for small gardens. Some are thugs, so stick to the smaller-growing, smaller-flowered types such as the bright yellow scented *Rhododendron luteum*.

Then you have the trees and shrubs with interesting bark or structures. The almost

A spring border featuring *Magnolia* ×*soulangeana* and an amelanchier underplanted with *Narcissus* 'Pipit', *Muscari*, *Daphne retusa*, Barnhaven primroses, *Osmanthus delavayi*, and *Lunaria annua* var. *albiflora* 'Alba Variegata'.

Rhododendron 'Olga Mezitt' with a *Primula sieboldii* hybrid growing in a garden in Canada.

white bark of the silver birch *Betula utilis* var. *jacquemontii* 'Grayswood Ghost' or the peeling bark of some maple varieties including *Acer capillipes* or *A. griseum* creates a dramatic backdrop for primroses. Underplant a row of red-twig dogwoods, *Cornus alba* 'Siberica', with *Primula* Cowichan Yellow Group for a stunning display.

In Brittany, France, where we grow primroses, hydrangeas are a staple plant in most gardens. Primroses readily colonize around the feet of these shrubs and provide early flowers under the bare shoots where they will be protected from the summer sun.

BULBS, TUBERS, AND CORMS

Spring is many people's favourite time of year and who can blame them when, against a backdrop of every kind of green hue, splashes of colour start to light up the bleak earth and the whole garden seems to burst into song. Essential players for an early spring display are, of course, the juliana primroses, acaulis, polyanthus, and *Primula denticulata*, but a host of other wonderful plants will combine with their glorious colours to make something special to look forward to in the winter months. Spring bulbs are an obvious choice as they provide a contrast of colours and form in both flowers and foliage. You will have to think about the right type of bulbs especially when it comes to the flowering times.

For early flowering in the garden, primroses, snowdrops, crocuses, and some miniature irises provide a splash of much-needed colour in late winter. Snowdrops naturalize beautifully and are easy to combine with many of the colours of the smaller acaulis and julianas.

Winter aconite (*Eranthis hyemalis*) starts lighting up the earth from late winter and enjoys conditions similar to those favoured by primroses, naturalizing under trees and banks. With its cheerful yellow cup-shaped flowers on ruffs of green foliage, winter aconite creates a welcome injection of colour when grown with some early flowering blue julianas.

Cyclamen coum is also one of the first plants to flower, often in late winter, and it too likes woodland conditions. It has lovely marbled, dark green or pewter leaves that offset the pink-and-white flowers beautifully. Because this species also likes dry conditions in summer, it is a good idea to plant it closer to tree roots where the soil is drier, with the primulas a bit further out. The cyclamen will self-sow profusely and eventually form a thick mat of leaves through which primroses will not grow. You have to be prepared to be ruthless.

Small *Iris reticulata* or the hybrids of *I. histrioides* can enhance an early display of acaulis primroses. The blues and purples of the irises combine wonderfully with pastel-coloured primroses in the Barnhaven Blues Group or the Candy Pinks Group. Ideally, the irises like a sunnier position than the primulas, but in a well-drained situation in dappled shade they should do well. The same can be said of scillas, which make up in colour what they lack in size; their vivid blue flowers are just stunning with white forms of *Primula vulgaris*.

There so many daffodils to choose from. Some of our firm favourites include the smaller-flowering, early varieties such as *Narcissus* 'Tête-à-Tête', *N.* 'Jetfire', or *N.* 'February Gold' that flower in early spring and complement the acaulis varieties beautifully.

For mid to late spring displays, you can choose from a whole range of daffodils, tulips, hyacinths, and other woodland natives. Beds of tulips underplanted with polyanthus primulas are often seen in town plantings. Although this regimented effect does not always suit smaller gardens, tulips can be very effective in a more natural bed. Try some of the later-flowering dark Cowichans with white tulips or primulas in the bright red Indian Reds Group with yellow tulips.

Leucojums are closely related to snowdrops but slightly later flowering. The tall stems of the former can lighten up the darker coloured primroses such as the Midnight Group, reflecting the white edges.

Who can resist a carpet of bluebells (or even just a small corner), flowering usually at a later time to some of the primroses? We have often grown them with white cultivars of *Primula sieboldii* such as Snowbird Group.

Grape hyacinths (*Muscari*) also flower around the time of most of the polyanthus and acaulis primroses. Today there are white and even pink varieties available. These tiny bulbs are a staple for container plantings and will multiply readily in a corner of the rock garden. We often use *M. ameniacum* with the creamy flowers of *Primula* Chartreuse Group.

Snake's head fritillary, or *Fritillaria meleagris*, with its white or purple flowers in midspring, also naturalizes in shady environments. For planting under deciduous trees, *Erythronium* (dog-tooth violet) is another genus of hardy spring-flowering perennials. It has long toothlike bulbs and produces spectacular flowers from early to midspring.

White acaulis primroses with snowdrops and hellebores at Dial Park in Chaddesley Corbett, Worcestershire, England.

ANNUALS

If you are planning on temporary spring beds or containers that include primulas, you may want to consider some of the following tried-and-tested combinations. Polyanthus are often grown in bedding displays with winter-flowering violas or pansies. Wallflowers (*Erysimum* species), although strictly biennials, are also still a reliable staple for town plantings and create very bright displays of yellow and red which can be combined with the bright red or yellow polyanthus for a midspring display. Like wallflowers, forget-me-nots (*Myosotis* species) self-seed reliably, creating a frothy blue backdrop every spring if you allow them to pop up all over your garden.

PERENNIALS

Hellebores are one of the first plants that come to mind when choosing companions for primroses. *Helleborus ×hybridus* cultivars are an especially good choice as the flowers appear in early spring before the new foliage when the tall stems will complement beautifully the lower-growing primulas, and then the leaves come into play and provide shady cover over the summer. Hellebores appreciate a cool position with sun in the morning but not in the afternoon, which suits the primroses perfectly.

For a woodland or area of dappled shade however big or small, you will find a lot of planting companions that make the most of the light in spring before the leaves cast their shade and will complement the midspring-flowering acaulis and polyanthus and *Primula sieboldii*.

Wood anemones (*Anemone nemorosa* or the American equivalent, *A. quinquefolia*) are among the first that come to mind with their brief but beautiful carpets of white and pink flowers. Sweet-smelling lily of the valley (*Convallaria majalis*) will also spread in a similar way on rhizomes to form extensive colonies; the lilies are easy to combine with many colours of polyanthus and the flowering often overlaps with *Primula sieboldii* hybrids. Many varieties of violets also create lovely a spring carpet.

For some height in shady sites, try the contrasting bleeding heart (*Dicentra* sp.). The heart-shaped flowers on long stems and the interesting foliage work well with *Primula sieboldii* hybrids as they flower in late spring. Try *D. spectabilis* 'Alba' with pink-flowering *P. sieboldii* 'Romance' or *P. sieboldii* 'Carefree'. Solomon's seal (*Polygonatum* sp.) can also

A bed in the Asian woods at Chanticleer garden in Pennsylvania features pink-and-white hybrids of *Primula sieboldii* floating about magically with yellow *Disporum flavens*, golden miniature hostas, and blue-flowering brunnera, creating a display that is to die for.

be used for a similar effect as a backdrop. We like *Polygonatum odoratum* 'Variegatum' for its ability to spread and the white edges on its leaves.

Brunneras have lovely foliage, often in shades of green and silver, that emerges in midspring. The plants love shady spots and their flowers are frothy blue or white sprays that look like forget-me-nots. *Brunnera* 'Jack Frost' is an especially outstanding variety with variegated foliage.

The spotted foliage of lungwort (*Pulmonaria saccharata*) is a great addition to any shady spring display. The midspring flowers are blue, purple, or pink, but it is really the foliage that is stunning. We especially like *P. saccharata* 'Silverado' with its large white silvery spots. You can also try epimediums, very gracious woodlanders with dainty spring flowers on wiry stems in a wide range of colours that often have very interesting marbled foliage.

We just love trilliums. These striking spring-flowering perennials spread on rhizomes and produce three leaves topped by a flower which ranges from white to dark red. They have to be planted en masse to be effective and need woodland shady conditions to thrive, but this native of North America is a stunner and will complement *Primula sieboldii* wonderfully. *Trillium cuneatum* grows 30–45 cm high and has the additional interest of marbled foliage.

Iris chrysographes with bright orange *Primula* 'Inverewe' (right), *P. ×bulleesiana* (pink), and *P. alpicola* (front) at Kevock Garden in Scotland.

For bog garden primulas such as the candelabras and the belled primulas, the most obvious companions are the water-loving irises, such as the flag irises or the native *Iris pseudacorus*, though the latter can be invasive. Japanese iris (*Iris ensata*) flowers at a similar time as the primulas and complements them, creating a glorious display. Siberian iris (*Iris siberica*) is also stunning next to the yellow flowers of *Primula prolifera*. Other moisture-loving perennials with very showy plumelike floral stems are astilbes. Ligularias also flower at the same time as candelabras and have striking spires of yellow or orange flowers in early to midsummer.

Meconopsis species (Himalayan blue poppy) only grow well in areas with plenty of snow cover in winter and relatively cool climates. If this is the case in your garden, you really must get hold of some of the perennial types such as *M. baileyi* or *M. grandis* and grow them with *Primula alpicola* or *P. ioessa* for a breathtaking display.

FOLIAGE PLANTS

Hostas feature prominently along with the *Primula japonica* hybrids in this garden in Ontario, Canada, where they grow in a ditch that becomes a runoff in spring or in heavy rains.

Grasses can create a wonderful background structure for perennial primroses. *Miscanthus* species, for example, grow well in partial shade and also form seed heads to create interest all through winter. Smaller grasses such as *Ophiopogon planiscapus* 'Nigrescens', with its dark leaves, offsets light pink *Primula* 'Kinlough Beauty' and complements some of the Gold-laced primulas. To brighten up a shady spot, nothing is better than the bright light green of Bowles' golden grass (*Milium effusum* 'Aureum') with some bright blue polyanthus.

For large imposing foliage plants on banks of streams and ponds, you can't go wrong with the dramatic leaves of *Gunnera manicata* surrounded by *Primula pulverulenta* or *P. japonica*, but bear in mind you may have to give the gunnera some winter protection and it needs lots and lots of water. *Astilboides tabularis* also has large luxurious foliage whose individual leaves can measure up to 28 in. (70 cm) in diameter. This herbaceous perennial likes moist well-drained soil and is often found planted with astilbes or rodgersias, some of which have very fetching dark foliage. *Cimicifuga atropurpurea* 'Brunette' (also known as *Actaea simplex* [Atropurpurea Group] 'Brunette') is another stunning perennial with dark brown foliage. Plant it with a group of white candelabras and it will take your breath away.

Many candelabras are grown at Kevock garden in Scotland, including bright orange *Primula* 'Inverewe', pinky purple *P. beesiana*, orange *P. bulleyana* and *P. ×bulleesiana* (visible at the back), and *P. pulverulenta* (on left).

Shade-loving hostas and ferns are great partners for many woodland areas and shady borders. They also do well as companions to the bog garden primulas, such as the candelabras or the later-flowering belled primulas and *Primula sieboldii*. The fern and hosta leaves will have just unfurled at the same time as the primulas come into flower and the fresh varied greens will grow up among the strong tall scapes of the flowers. Try dark green *Hosta* 'Snowden' with *P. japonica* 'Miller's Crimson' or *P. pulverulenta*.

Heucheras also thrive in partial shade and make great companions for primulas in containers as the foliage is stunning in late spring and then the flowers will take over when the primulas have stopped in early to late summer. We love the purple-foliaged *Heuchera* 'Plum Pudding' with *Primula* 'Guinevere'.

ALPINE PLANTS

Many alpine plants grow with Border auriculas, *Primula marginata*, and *P. allionii* hybrids. It is hard to name only a few, but saxifrages, sedums, and sempervivums create very interesting displays.

John Richards, author of the botanical guide to *Primula*, likes growing his alpines in troughs. Some of his favourite companions are saxifrages, with an interesting evergreen foliage which looks lovely in early spring. He particularly recommends the silver forms that have large panicles of flowers in early summer such as the hybrids of *Saxifraga cochlearis*, *S. crustata*, *S. paniculata*, and *S. hostii*. He also uses the porophyllum saxifrages that flower in spring, especially species such as *S. ferdinandi-coburgii* or *S. marginata*, which are more persistent than many newer hybrids. Golden oldies such

Primula marginata (left) and *P.* 'Hyacinthia' with saxifrages growing in a stone trough.

as *S*. 'Gregor Mendel' with its pale yellow flowers in early spring or *S*. 'Johan Kellerer', which has pale pink flowers, also do well in the open garden.

We could continue as there are so many other plants that come to mind and that we have seen growing wonderfully in other gardens but we can't list them all. So be inspired, ask at your local nursery for other shade- and moisture-loving plants, visit some show gardens in spring and take their ideas home with you.

Container Arrangements

Nearly all primulas are well-suited to container planting. It is a great way to bring these plants to the forefront when they are at their best and they can make a stunning display planted on their own or with other plants. It is also a great solution for people who don't have a garden as container plants can be grown on balconies and window-ledges, or even in cold conservatories. As long as you choose the right container for the right plant and place it in a cool shady position, it is a very easy way to bring spring up close and personal.

Some primulas are just so special they certainly will benefit from being put on show when they are at their peak to bring out the "wow" factor. Of course, they can be planted in containers that can be placed strategically near a door or window in the spring and then tucked away in a shady place for the rest of the year.

CHOICE OF CONTAINER

The choice of container will depend on the chosen plant variety. We use a lot of zinc tubs for our displays (with holes drilled in the bottom) as the colour seems to off-set primulas really well. Old white sinks, stone troughs, window boxes, old wooden boxes, clay pots, plastic pots in bright colours—as long as there is room for the roots and good drainage, most containers will work for primulas. Have a look round a flea-market and see what you can find.

Most primroses, polyanthus, julianas, and double primroses are at home in small pots. They are well suited to window boxes and larger pots in combination with other plants. Try lining a basket with plastic, make a few slits in the base for drainage, and place double primroses in it to create a lovely old-fashioned display for a windowsill or even table decoration.

Some plants will need fairly large pots at least 24 in. (60 cm) deep to accommodate their long fleshy roots. Candelabras or denticulatas are among them. Remember that primulas from this group will also need a lot of watering. Alpines and auriculas will do better in small pots, where their roots are constricted and the plants themselves need

A trio of Belarina double primroses in a basket: Buttercup Yellow, Nectarine, and Cream.

Border auriculas in clay pot.

a lot less looking after. Keep in mind that they will need to be protected from excess moisture in the winter unless you live in an area that gets good snow cover. Some people protect them by placing sheets of polythene balanced on rocks, but if the the plants are in small pots the easiest thing is to move them to a choice spot where they don't get too wet, such as a windowsill or a sheltered corner against a wall.

Auriculas are traditionally grown in clay pots or long toms which taper at the end to allow very good drainage and good root development; however, these do tend to dry out much faster than plastic pots.

Hybrids of *Primula sieboldii* are also traditionally shown in black or brown glazed pots but again, unless you are going to be showing plants, why not simply be inventive? In Japan, these hybrids are grown mainly as pot plants and you will see many lining the streets with their bright blooms in late spring. Although they are a great garden plant, they are also very showy and can look great close up. They have a shallow rooting system so can be grown in relatively small pots and they will need tucking back into bed sometimes over the winter as they have a tendency to try and climb out of their pots.

Stone troughs are a very suitable and effective way for growing many primulas unless you live in a hot climate in which case the plants may dry out too quickly. Of course, if

Containers with *Primula sieboldii* hybrids line a fence.

Primula Gold-laced Group with *P.* Harvest Yellow Group in an old sink.

Showy *Primula* Gold-laced Group with *Narcissus* 'Tête à Tête' and *Ophiopogon planiscapus* 'Nigrescens' in an attention-getting container.

you can get hold of an original stone drinking trough that's ideal, but they are becoming harder to get hold of and so an interesting alternative is to make your own trough using hypertufa. Fill your pot with a suitable mix of gravelly compost, add a few rocks, and you have a very authentic planter ready to grow auriculas or alpine primulas.

CHOICE OF PLANT

Although all primulas are good container plants, some are showier than others and lend themselves to being placed in a highly visible spot. Among these are the Gold-laced or anomalous primroses that would perhaps be lost in the garden. In a container close to the house, they can be shown off to their best advantage and admired close up. Imagine how lovely a bright yellow container filled with Gold-laced primula, a yellow daffodil, and black mondo grass would look placed by a front door step or on a garden table.

A pot of the more unusual forms such as Hose-in-hose or Jack-in-the-Green would also be a good talking point. Double primroses are well suited to this kind of treatment and look stunning on their own in a pot or a series of pots of the same colour. Container plantings are a good way to keep an eye on some of the smaller plants and to ensure that alpines and auriculas grow in the best conditions.

DESIGNING WITH POTS

There are so many ways to arrange pots. They can be placed on an outside windowsill, on a shady balcony grouped with several other pots, or on an outside table, to name a few.

Auriculas are by nature a showy flower and therefore lend themselves so well to some wonderful displays, as anyone who has been to the Chelsea Flower Show will have seen. However, it is possible for anyone to replicate this on a smaller scale at home. Keeping pots on a north- or east-facing windowsill is a simple way of putting plants on display.

The traditional way to display auriculas is in "theatres" that offer a little protection from the rain so that it doesn't wash off the farina on the leaves. Often this involves placing potted plants in shelves on a wall, but there are so many innovative ways of displaying plants. How about placing plants on an old ladder or on a repainted, old bookshelf? Simply putting a few shelves up on the outside of your potting shed can be very effective.

For a formal effect, try planting two large pots on either side of the door with evergreen shrubs such as skimmia or boxwood and incorporate acaulis primroses at the base. Primroses can also be very effective in formal urns.

Where space is limited, such as for urban gardeners with a small balcony, it is possible to create a miniature spring garden by growing primroses in half barrels. These containers give plenty of space to add lots of companion plants such as hellebores to create height and even small shrubs.

A mixture of Belarina double primroses (Cobalt Blue, Pink Ice, Buttercup Yellow, Cream, and Nectarine) with ivy and *Skimmia japonica*.

A simple way of displaying auriculas on an old ladder.

Auriculas displayed on simple shelving by Pat and Robin Fisher, holders of a National Plant Collection of Border auriculas.

Primula Innisfree with *Muscari*.

Narcissus 'Jenny', *Epimedium* 'Spine Tingler', and sedge (*Carex*) with *Primula* Spice Shades Group in an old zinc pot.

COMPANIONS FOR POTS

Think about combining your primulas in a pot with plants that will extend the flowering time of the display. Why not plant a series of staggered flowering bulbs with early flowers, such as small *Narcissus* 'Jenny', and with later-flowering tulips? Introducing some foliage such as ferns or grasses will shade the primulas later in the season and provide longer interest and height.

We love combining euphorbia with dark red polyanthus. Some of the smaller spring-flowering bulbs such as muscari are particularly suited to planting in small pots. Try blue muscari with double primrose 'Petticoat'. Simply grouping spring-flowering plants together in separate pots can also be very effective. We also love the idea of a miniature bog garden in an old tin bath using candelabra primulas with other bog garden plants.

Euphorbia Redwing 'Charam' with *Primula* Tartan Reds Group and *P.* Harbour Lights mixture.

Primulas in the Wildlife Garden

Most types of primulas are attractive to mason bees, honeybees, solitary bees, bumble-bees, butterflies, and bee fly (*Bombylius major*). The flowers are a real boon for early pollinators when not much else is in bloom. As the insects come out of their winter hibernation, they need to find pollen and nectar to help them survive. The first flowers to appear each spring are especially valued since they help to establish a resident bee population which is needed throughout the growing season.

Primula vulgaris and a common bee fly.

If you are looking for plants that attract insects, choose the single-flowering primroses and polyanthus and the julianas. Later in the season, the candelabra and belled primulas are particularly appealing.

Both species of wild *Primula* commonly found in the British countryside, the cowslip (*P. veris*) and primrose (*P. vulgaris*), are used as caterpillar food-plants by the endangered Duke of Burgundy butterfly. Considerable efforts are being made to help this fast-declining species, and some conservation projects have involved the propagation of *Primula* for subsequent transplantation into areas of potentially suitable habitat for the butterfly, where the plants are rare or even absent. It is illegal to dig up wild primroses, so the best way to obtain your own plants is to sow seed of *P. veris* or *P. vulgaris* that comes from a reputable source.

Mating pair of Duke of Burgundy butterflies, sitting on one of its caterpillar food-plants, cowslip (*Primula veris*).

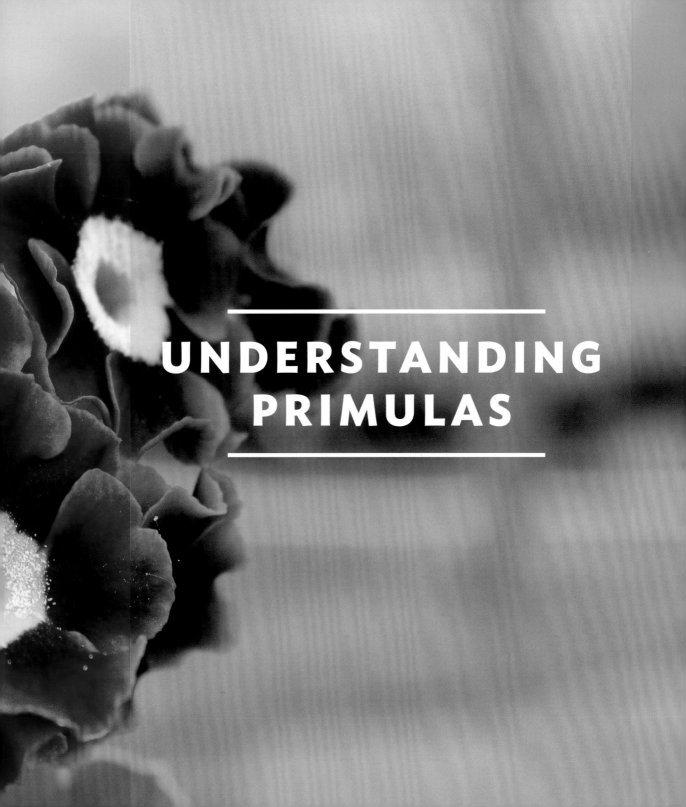

UNDERSTANDING PRIMULAS

The genes of *Primula juliae* can be found in most of the modern hybrids.

T

The genus *Primula* is composed of approximately 430 species spread in various habitats throughout the Northern Hemisphere. It is one of the largest, most diverse and widespread genera and a fascinating group for botanists, collectors, and researchers. This explains why there have been so many detailed studies and books based on these plants.

While there are many knowledgeable experts and collectors who will happily discuss in minute detail the classification of the species and the exact origins of cultivars, the average gardener does not need to have a lot of botanical knowledge to grow the many primulas that are well suited to cultivation. However, without getting too technical, there are some interesting facts about the species in this book that may help you understand a bit more about growing them (or at least be useful when trying to impress your gardening friends).

Types of *Primula*

The genus *Primula* is part of the family Primulaceae, which surprisingly includes the genera *Soldanella* and *Cyclamen*. Botanists have grouped *Primula* species into 37 sections based on similarities in leaf, flower, and general habit. This botanical classification has been regularly updated over the centuries, especially recently with the new knowledge about genetics. Classification information is helpful to the gardener as it gives clues as to how to cultivate the plants in the garden.

To help you understand the different types of primula that exist, we have grouped the plants into categories. This is not a botanical classification; rather, we have grouped plants that have similar growing habits and similar uses in the garden. These are the groups that are often used commercially and may help you find your way around nurseries or online resources.

Primroses and polyanthus All the primroses and hybrids that resemble the common English primrose (*Primula vulgaris*) or cowslip (*P. veris*). They come in all the colours of the rainbow and have either low-flowering or taller-flowering habits. You will recognize them from the familiar leaves.

Double primroses The common primrose form, but the flowers have several extra layers of petals.

Juliana primroses Hybrids of *Primula juliae*, also known as Julianas, Wandas, or Pruhonicians (*P. ×pruhoniciana*). Lower growing than the common primrose, they also have rounder leaves. Originally native to the Caucasus.

Unusual forms Also known as anomalous primroses or Elizabethan primroses. They are primroses and polyanthus forms that have mutated so that the flowers take on strange and unusual forms.

Candelabras Japanese primrose (*Primula japonica*) and other species whose flowers appear in circles set at intervals up the stem, somewhat resembling an old-fashioned candlestick. They require constant moisture and are often referred to as bog primulas or sometimes woodland primula.

Belled primulas Includes primulas with gently drooping bell-like flowers. They are also often classed as bog primulas.

***Primula sieboldii* hybrids** Cultivars and hybrids of Japanese woodland *Primula sieboldii* that has slightly hairy leaves and a creeping habit.

Alpine primulas Hybrids and species of *Primula* native to the European Alps which are low-growing rock plants.

Auriculas Cultivars and hybrids of *Primula auricula*. They have showy flowers and glossier, rounder leaves than the common primrose.

Floral Morphology

Primroses have a very distinctive reproduction system and are often used as examples in school biology books to illustrate how plants reproduce. The vast majority of species are heterostylous, that is, they have flowers with styles of two different lengths, although

A Presidential Primrose

PRIMULA 'MONEYGALL' WAS NAMED in honour of the maternal ancestral village of American President Barack Obama and was gifted to him and Mrs. Obama during their state visit to Ireland by Irish Prime Minister Enda Kenny and his wife on St. Patrick's Day 2013. It has a similar colour and habit to *P. vulgaris* with slightly darker leaves. It is unusual in that it has a mix of hose-in-hose and single flowers on polyanthus stems. It is a result of Joe Kennedy's breeding programme in Ireland.

the flowers on one plant will always be of the same kind. The two flower forms are very easy to observe on the acaulis primroses. Flowers are either pin form, in which case the stigma which receives the pollen is visible above the anthers which carry the pollen, or they are thrum form, in which case the anthers are visible at the mouth of the flower and the stigma is lower down.

Having flowers with two types of styles means that before such a primrose can produce seed, a bee or other insect has to pass pollen from the anthers of a pin flower onto the stigma of a thrum flower or vice-versa. This set-up avoids self-pollination, which tends to lead to a degeneration of the flowers. If you want your plants to set seed in the garden, you will need to grow them in groups, as an individual plant will rarely set viable seed. It also means that in general any viable seed will have come from a cross with another plant.

Two different types of flowers. The thrum form is on the left and the pin form on the right.

Ripe seed pod.

After fertilization, the seeds are formed in the ovary. When the seeds are ripe, a small bubble of air pushes open the top (or the side on some species) of the seed pod. The seed is then shaken to the ground by the wind or spread by animals such as birds and mice.

The best time to harvest seed for most species is when it is ripe and the seeds turn brown. They can then be sown immediately if so wished and if you can keep the germinating seedlings cool enough. However, in the wild many species germinate after a period of cold, when the snow melts and the ground warms up. This can be reproduced by keeping the seeds in the refrigerator until they are ready to be sown.

Origin

Knowing where plants grow in the wild can help gardeners better understand their needs in cultivation. Over 90 percent of *Primula* species are native to the Himalayas and western China, where there are surely more species waiting to be discovered in remote areas. To put this into perspective, out of the 430 *Primula* species worldwide, only 34 are from Europe and 20 from North America.

Most species come from cooler regions, often mountainous areas that are used to snow cover, but there are also some surprising species that grow in warmer climates. One of these is *Primula palinuri*, found in southwestern Italy on maritime cliffs.

Some very beautiful species are hard to maintain in cultivation and should be left to experienced growers who can try to replicate a plant's native conditions in an alpine house, but many species readily adapt to garden culture as long as their basic needs are met.

Introduction into Cultivation

So how did these wild species come into our gardens? The first mention of primroses dates back to John Gerard's *Herbal* of 1597, which describes plants with medicinal value. Gerard references green primroses, hose-in-hose forms, cowslips, and "Our Garden Double primrose" as if they were already common indeed in gardens.

The introduction of *Primula auricula* into cultivation owes a lot to sixteenth-century botanist Carolus Clusius. From that time onward, auriculas were cultivated in Europe. While the Europeans were breeding primrose and auricula hybrids, the Japanese were developing some of their own natives such as *P. sieboldii* of which many forms were introduced into cultivation. Originally from light woodland and damp meadowlands in Japan, eastern Siberia, Korea, and Manchuria, *P. sieboldii* was introduced to Europe by Philipp F. von Siebold in the nineteenth century and is now considered an endangered species in many places.

The nineteenth century was the age of the great botanical expeditions of Europeans into the relatively unknown western Himalaya and the expansion of the seed firms that financed the famous collectors. Joseph Hooker collected for Kew Gardens in the 1840s, hunting for plants in the Himalayas, Sikkim, and northern India. Among his many introductions were *Primula involucrata*, *P. sikkimensis* and *P. capitata*. What an exciting time it must have been for the western explorers discovering for the first time the diversity of flora of these regions. Many of the people who discovered the plants have left their legacy in the name of the plants such as *P. sieboldii* or *P. wilsonii* or the impossible-to-pronounce *P. maximowizcii*.

French missionaries to western China were responsible for much of the early botanical work in that area. Jean Delavay, for one, found *Primula secundiflora* in Yunnan province. Plant hunting was not an easy task, and there are many wild tales of collectors being shot at by religious fanatics or fleeing for their lives and having to leave their collections behind.

George Forrest, an Englishman supported financially by Arthur Bulley, a Lancashire cotton millionaire who ran a seed company called Bees seeds, collected plants in China from 1904 to 1932 and was responsible for introducing such gems as *Primula beesiana* and *P. bulleyana*.

It is impossible to name all the collectors and researchers who have contributed to introducing and recording the numerous *Primula* species. This work continues today with botanists such as Pam Eveleigh who is compiling an electronic database of all the species on her website Primula World and who has travelled with David and Stella Rankin of Kevock Gardens to China to clear up the identification of *P. bracteata* and *P. bullata*.

Isn't it interesting to imagine that on one spring day of about one hundred and fifty years ago Japanese samurais were sitting and enjoying *Primula sieboldii* over a cup of green tea exactly when English gentlemen were sitting and talking about Auriculas over a cup of tea?

—EXTRACT FROM HAND-TYPED INTRODUCTORY NOTES FOUND IN A COPY OF *SAKURASŌ* (*P. SIEBOLDII* E. MORREN) WRITTEN BY KAZUO HARA OF THE MATSUMOTO SAKURASŌ AND PRIMULA CLUB.

From a collector's point of view, how plants came into cultivation from the wild and how they were and are cultivated in our changing societies reflect so many of the historical changes over the last centuries and is absolutely thrilling. Growing some of the old varieties and species is like having a piece of history growing in your garden.

The Auriculas

Primula auricula has an astonishing story. The plant has been revered by florists and painters, botanists and amateur gardeners, displayed in theatres, and has been the object of fierce competitions. It has been grown by kings and duchesses as well as weavers and miners. Fashions in plants come and go, and although auriculas have been very popular in England for years, the number of auricula collectors is again on the increase worldwide. An auricula display in full bloom still has the power to stop young and old in their tracks—but its history is just as fascinating as the flowers themselves.

Pam Eveleigh in Yunnan, China, in a mixed field of *Primula secundiflora* and *P. sikkimensis*.

Native Species to Look For in the Wild

IN THE UNITED KINGDOM
Primula vulgaris (common primrose)
Primula veris (cowslip)
Primula elatior (oxlip)
Primula scotica (Scottish primrose)
Primula farinosa (bird's-eye primrose)—mainly in
 Scotland

IN THE UNITED STATES
Primula parryi (Parry's primrose)
Primula mistassinica (bird's-eye primrose)

IN CANADA
Primula mistassinica (dwarf Canadian primrose)
Primula laurentiana (bird's-eye primrose)

Primula elatior, the true oxlip, is rarely found in the wild apart from a few woods in East Anglia, England. Visually, it combines the virtues of both cowslip and primrose and is a very good indicator of ancient woodland, so a sighting is to be treasured. You can tell it apart from *P. veris* (cowslip) in that it has larger flowers that droop to one side and the flowers don't have the telltale red dots inside. The flowers are usually a pale yellow.

Despite their exotic appearance, the auriculas we grow today are descendants of native European primulas mainly from the Alps. Some hybrids produce a protective layer, technically called a farina, or meal, which gives a white or sometimes yellowy, waxy or powdery aspect to some of the leaves and flowers. This farina protects the plant from the sun at high altitude and is actually a very fine layer of microscopic hairs. People unfamiliar with it sometimes express concern that the plant is unhealthy, but on the contrary, in the auricula world it is often seen as a very desirable characteristic.

Farina on Auricula leaves can give them a white powdery aspect.

Primula auricula in the wild is yellow with varying amounts of farina.

The name *Primula auricula* stems from the vernacular name of bear's ears, referring to the shape of the leaf. Our modern-day auricula originally came from a cross between the wild *P. auricula* and *P. hirsuta*. The huge range of colours and forms can be explained by the yellow, pink, and red genes inherited from the original parents, but probably other *Primula* varieties have also contributed to the genetic make-up of this group. The amazing perfection of the flowers has been achieved by patient hybridizers over the centuries who still strive today to breed ever-improved varieties.

AURICULA HISTORY

Herbalists first mentioned auriculas in the late fifteenth century. Originating from mountainous areas of Austria and Switzerland, these plants were reputed to cure nausea and vertigo.

The sixteenth century was the time of plant hunters and botanical expeditions. One of the most important botanical writers of the era was Charles de l'Ecluse, or Clusius, imperial court botanist in Vienna for Emperor Maximilian II. While in Vienna, Clusius visited his friend Johannes Aichholtz, a professor and the proud owner of two apparently different types of auricula—one yellow (which he called Auricula Ursi I) and the other pink (Auricula Ursi II), which turned out to be the *P. hirsuta* hybrid. Clusius mentioned that the local herb woman gathered roots and flowers to sell in the Viennese market, many of which were apparently bought by Viennese ladies to plant in their gardens.

Enthusiasm for floriculture spread rapidly across Europe and people were looking out for new and attractive plants. From the beginning of the seventeenth century, there is a marked preference for the different colour hybrids over the wild yellow form. This is the time of the *curieux* (also called florists), who collected and strived to improve the different plants. Because of its fascinating ability to produce a wide variety of forms and colours, the auricula became one of the treasured florist flowers (along with roses, tulips, and others). Commercial nurseries started to develop and auriculas appeared in nursery catalogues. In 1610, Conrad Sweert, a Dutch florist with a business in Frankfurt am Main in Germany, offered six varieties for sale. A huge number of *florilegium* (flower anthologies) were produced, one of which was *Hortus Eystettensis*, prepared in 1613 for Johann Conrad, Prince Bishop of Eichstatt, by the apothecary Basilus Besler and featuring three auriculas.

The stand erected by the Northern Section of the National Auricula and Primula Society at one of the Harrogate Spring Flower Shows.

Around this time, auriculas began to be displayed in "theatres" painted black, often with curtains and mirrors. It is difficult to say where this tradition began, but Charles Géunin in his book of 1732 mentions the town of Tournai in Wallonia, Belgium, where the Abbot of Saint Michel had 15 auricula theatres on display.

Toward the end of the eighteenth century, there was an auriculamania in the lowlands of Europe that almost reached the proportions of tulipomania. Doubles were especially prized and sold for a lot of money. In 1799 in Meissen, Germany, Franz August Kanngiesser published an *Aurikelflora* containing coloured illustrations of 144 cultivars. In Germany and Wallonia, auricula societies began to appear and a specialist magazine even mentioned thefts of prize-winning auriculas. By the end of the eighteenth century, the Dutch city of Leiden was commercializing over 1000 different cultivars. From 1850 onward, they fell out of fashion. However, on the other side of the channel it was a different story.

The appearance of the auricula in England is often attributed to its arrival with Flemish weavers from 1570 and Huguenots from 1620 to 1685 who were fleeing religious persecution. Florist societies, first created in 1630, played a major role in popularizing auriculas in the seventeenth and eighteenth centuries. The plants became associated with northern miners who organized feasts in public houses—the prize for best in show often being a copper kettle.

In southern England, the upper classes held numerous collections in their stately homes, and specialized nurseries sold cultivars at high prices. Somewhat neglected during the Industrial Revolution and with the arrival of exotic plants for the heated glasshouse, auriculas regained popularity around 1870. Many cultivars disappeared during the two world wars, but horticultural societies such as the National Auricula and Primula Society founded in 1873 and some amateur growers kept the flame alive. Auriculas are still a popular flower, often making an impressive appearance at Chelsea Flower Show.

As to how and when auriculas were introduced in the New World, it is quite likely that Thomas Jefferson, American envoy to France in 1785, came across some of the *curieux fleuristes* in Europe. A plant enthusiast himself, he mentions auriculas in his writings and took plants and seed back to the States and grew them with varying success.

In the 1893 World Columbian Exposition in Chicago, auriculas figured on a list of old-fashioned cottage garden flowers. The American Primrose Society was founded in 1941 as interest grew supported by Florence Bellis, editor for many years of the *American Primrose Society Journal*. This society is still very much alive, and many amateur growers are producing some wonderful auriculas today.

With the help of florists' societies, people are still growing and showing these fascinating plants all over the world. Regular competitions are held with very strict rules about show categories that date back to the time of the early florists. Since the 1960s, double auriculas have been revived and exciting new stripes are being developed. In recent years they have been reappearing on gardening programmes. Slowly but surely people are building collections, swapping with other growers, posting pictures on blogs, taking part in forums with people from all over the world, creating pinterest pages. The great auricula digital revival is here. Who knows what exciting new plants will appear and which direction breeding will take. What's for sure is that we haven't heard the last of them yet.

The auricula theatre at Calke Abbey dates back to the eighteenth century.

Sakurasō

THE JAPANESE HAVE BRED AND CULTIVATED *sakurasō* (cherry blossom primrose, or *Primula sieboldii*) to dizzy heights only comparable to that of *P. auricula* in Western Europe. The first mention of its cultivation is found in the first gardening book published in Japan in 1681. It was during the Edo period, when wealthy merchants and samurai started to grow primulas as pot plants. Societies devoted to their culture were established and in 1804 the first flower show for new introductions of sakurasō was held. The plant became very popular with many gardeners from all social classes, and 88 cultivars were illustrated in the *Sakurasō Kahinzen* published in 1812.

After the Edo era, interest in cultivation of plants declined. Many named varieties were lost at this time. The aristocratic classes managed to maintain some of the sakurasō groups although it was not until 1918 that Nihon Sakurasō Kai (Japanese Sakurasō Society) was launched. Unlike the earlier societies, it held public flower shows at which the plants were shown in a traditional bamboo theatre called a *kadan*.

Like Show auriculas, primroses in Japan were classified into different groups mainly according to the overall form of the flower, the edges of the petals, the shape of the petals, how flat or drooping they are, and the different colour shadings on the flowers. One Japanese book goes so far as to detail the width of the flowers down to the nearest millimetre.

The societies were not able to continue during the Second World War but in spite of many plants being lost in air raids, enough remained for Sakurasō Kai to be re-launched in 1952. In recent years, *Primula sieboldii* cultivars have become popular again and there are three societies dedicated to their cultivation. The Research Centre of Agriculture and Forestry at the University of Tsukuba has set up a preservation programme aiming to safeguard more than 300 varieties.

Sakurasō Kadan
This style of display stand dates back to the 1840s and was carefully structured to enhance the beauty of *Primula sieboldii* cultivars on show. The stands are still used today at flower shows. This particular photo shows an elegant recreation of a traditional Kadan with five tiers. Plants are displayed in 33–38 traditional ceramic pots with the flowers alternating in colour and shape for an aesthetically pleasing display.

Auricula Types

Auricula exhibitions are held in the United Kingdom and the United States to display these wonderful plants and much literature has been written about them. To a novice it can all seem a bit bewildering and maybe off-putting, but you don't need to know a lot to grow them. Because they were grown as a florist's flower, they are classified into different categories and named according to strict rules. However without getting into all the ins and outs of showing plants, we will try to give you a brief overview of the different types without being too technical.

Border auriculas are bred to be tough garden plants that can withstand most weather conditions. They come in many shapes and forms and are reasonably indestructible when planted in the right place. The original wild species came from mountainous regions, which means that auriculas tolerate fierce winters especially when blanketed in snow. They have tough fleshy leaves that can be powdery and the flowers are usually quite scented. Great in the garden and in large containers, Border auriculas are good plants to begin with.

Primula auricula 'Rouge Gorge', a typical Border auricula with large frilly blooms and slightly notched petals.

Alpine auriculas can be recognized by the shading on the flower. They are usually darker near the centre, becoming lighter coloured toward the outside. They are without farina and, compared to Border auriculas, have very flat, round petals. The flowers are subdivided into two colour groups: those with light centres and those with gold centres. Light centres are usually shades of near blue, red becoming pink, or purple turning to mauve. Gold centres are generally dark red turning to bright red or are brown turning to gold. The flowers are large but usually are not as scented as the Border auriculas. Alpine auriculas are fairly easy-to-grow plants. They are often seen on the show bench but will do very well in the garden.

Primula auricula 'Piers Telford', a gold-centred alpine.

Primula auricula 'Adrian', a light-centred alpine.

Primula auricula 'Marie-Pierre', a double auricula.

Double auriculas have been making a comeback since the second half of the twentieth century. They now are available in a huge array of colours and forms and surprisingly are usually very scented. There are even some striped doubles today. Double auriculas are generally easy to grow in the garden or in pots.

Show Self auriculas are a single uniform colour with a circle of white paste in the centre. They are usually red, yellow, auricula blue, which is really a kind of purple, and very dark red where the colour is so concentrated the flower appears black. There are also some new colours beginning to appear. Some of the Show Selfs have very powdery leaves that can appear almost silver.

Striped auriculas were highly prized in the seventeenth and eighteenth centuries, but fell out of fashion when the Edged auriculas appeared. After being lost to cultivation for over 100 years, Striped auriculas became popular again in the twentieth century and returned to

Primula auricula 'Belle Zana', a pink Show Self.

the show bench in the 1970s. The stripes consist of farina on coloured petals, but some other different colour petal combinations are starting to reappear and also some double striped flowers. Plants are usually grown under protection from winter wet, but as a group tend to be quite vigorous, easy plants.

Show Edged auriculas are considered the ultimate collectors' plants and the aristocrats of the auricula world. The green edges on some plants are actually the result of a mutation of the petal into leaf material. This trait appeared in about 1740 and has since been bred into the flowers mainly by English hybridizers. You can now find green edges, grey edges (where the green edge is covered in white farina), and white edges (where the green edge is covered with so much farina that the petals appear white). A well-grown Edged auricula has a certain fascinating, almost artificial quality about it and can be very striking. Plants in this group are much sought after. It can be tricky to get show standard flowers on some of the cultivars, but many growers consider it well worth the effort.

Primula auricula 'Königin der Nacht', a Striped auricula.

Primula auricula 'Oban', a green-edged Show auricula.

Primula auricula 'Hawkwood', a Show Fancy auricula.

Show Fancy auriculas are edged varieties in the Show category that do not meet the strict criteria for the Edged auriculas. They still have the ring of paste in the centre and a green, grey, or white edge to the petals, but the main body colour is not black. Instead, it may be red, yellow, brown, or even pink.

There are over a thousand named cultivars of Show auriculas with new ones coming on to the market all the time, though some of these are not readily available. For this book, we have chosen cultivars in each category that are easy to grow and fairly easy to obtain just to give a snapshot of what is available. The best way to find out about plants is to talk to the specialist growers at nurseries and plant fairs or join one of the primula and auricula societies. You will notice that the grower or the person who raised the plant is mentioned in the description. This is valued information to growers as traditionally a plant needs to win a prize at a show to be named and propagated, and the information about the origins of a plant is considered very important to the collector.

100 PRIMULAS FOR THE GARDEN

PRIMROSES AND POLYANTHUS

This group, known as Vernales primulas, includes the common or English primrose (*Primula vulgaris*), cowslip (*P. veris*), oxlip (*P. elatior*), and all the thousands of hybrids resulting from these original wild plants. Flowers in this group come in two forms. In the acaulis form, the flowers are borne on individual short stems as in *P. vulgaris*. In the poly-anthus forms, several flowers are carried on an umbel on one tall stem. Polyanthus forms are also sometimes called bunch-flowering primroses or marketed as *P. elatior* (though this name should be reserved for the true oxlip species).

Most of the primroses on the market originated from crosses from these original species but many also contain genes from *Primula juliae* and other species. These are some of the earliest flowering, most widespread and commonly grown primroses. Hundreds are brought onto the market each year in all colours of the rainbow. It would be impossible to list even a fraction of them and even if we did the list would soon be out of date. Some of the commercial primroses that you will find in local garden centres have their place as annual spring flowers but are not always bred to be hardy and often sacrifice scent and colour for uniformity of growth. There are, however, plenty of very tough primulas available which will bloom year after year in the garden if planted in the right place and given a bit of care and attention. We have chosen to focus on a few of our favourite hardy primroses that are special to us, most of which have stood the test of time and are easily available.

Primroses can be used in many ways in the spring garden. They look good in small groups at the edge of a border, mixed with other spring-flowering perennials and bulbs or on their own. They can be grown in a shady rock garden, woodland garden, or by streams and can be used in formal or informal planting designs. The opportunities are limitless. They are very well suited to being grown in containers as their roots are not very long and they are quite happy in confined spaces. Many are highly scented and are a boon for attracting early insects.

Primula vulgaris
Wild primrose, English primrose
SYNONYM *P. acaulis*

This is the wild primrose native to many European countries and often known as the harbinger of spring. It is among the most-loved and well-known flowers in the countries where it grows in the wild. The pale yellow flower with a deep yellow centre seems to glow when seen in the evening light.

ZONES 3–9

HABIT AND SIZE Acaulis form. In the right conditions, it forms a good clump and readily self-seeds and even can be seen as invasive in some gardens. On a trip down to the Lyon area of southern France one spring, we saw lawns turned into carpets of stunning yellow. People just happily mow them and the flowers grow back again. Stem height 4 in. (10 cm).

FLOWERING Late winter to midspring.

CULTIVATION It seems to like fertile heavy (clay) soils in which it puts up with a fair amount of drying out in the summer.

ORIGIN It appears in the wild throughout Europe from southern Norway, the British Isles, and France to northern Africa, where it is one of the few native primroses. Like most primroses it favours cool damp places and is often seen growing in open woodland and north-facing grasslands, on banks and even on cliffs and mountain sides. In some parts of Britain it grew quite scarce as it was often dug up to be planted in gardens or sold in markets. So please don't dig up the wild ones—not only is it illegal in many countries, but you will contribute to the species dying out in the wild.

LANDSCAPE AND DESIGN USES A must-have plant for anyone trying to create a natural or cottage garden. It is also great for attracting insects as it is pollinated not only by bees but also by butterflies and long-tongued insects such as bee-flies and moths.

SIMILAR PLANTS There are other yellow acaulis primroses on the market but none can match the simple charm of the native species. *Primula* Barnhaven Gold Group is a darker yellow. *Primula* 'Maisie Michael' has soft-yellow flowers on dusky pink stems and its leaves have a reddish brown tinge.

Primula veris ▾

Cowslip, Culver keys, St. Peter's keys

A well-known, fairly common wild species in the United Kingdom and the rest of Europe. The fragrant flowers are fairly small, funnel shaped, and have characteristic orange spots at the base of the lobes. It is a species that will freely self-seed in the garden, so you will have to dead-head it if you don't want it to spread too much.

ZONES 3–9

HABIT AND SIZE Forms large-leaved plants and taller flower stems when growing in tall grass but low-lying rosettes 10 in. (25 cm) across when grown in an open bed. Stem height 4–12 in. (10–30 cm).

FLOWERING Slightly later than *P. vulgaris* and many other hybrids.

ORIGIN In Germany, cowslip is referred to as *schlüsselblume* or "key flower." The drooping flower clusters are said to resemble a bunch of keys, a symbol associated with St. Peter. The story goes that St. Peter found out that people were getting into heaven by a back way and became so agitated that he dropped his keys which turned into cowslips when they fell to the ground. In the wild, the species is generally found in open sunny places such as meadows and rail embankments, particularly on limestone or chalk soils.

LANDSCAPE AND DESIGN USES As they flower slightly later, cowslips are a great choice for growing with tulips or other spring-flowering bulbs and ferns. They are very attractive to pollinating insects, particularly bees. You can also use them in your bunches of spring flowers as they are great for cutting.

SIMILAR PLANTS There are several different coloured hybrids of the cowslip on the market in various shades of red ▶, orange, and yellow such as *P. veris* 'Sunset Shades' or *P.* 'Coronation Cowslips', which tend to be more vigorous and larger flowering plants. You will also find a double form called *P. veris* 'Katy McSparron' or a hose-in-hose strain called *P. veris* Lady Agatha Group, which seem to be just as vigorous as the single-flowered wild form.

Primula Barnhaven Blues Group

This is a seed strain which therefore shows some variation in colour ranging from dark blue to delicate light blue shades. Some plants are edged with white and are lightly scented. All are as reliable as the common primrose, *P. vulgaris*, and share the same vigorous habit. They have a very early and long flowering season. In the right spot they often flower again in the autumn if the conditions are right. The single flowers attract many pollinators, but watch out for birds who seem to particularly like blue flowers.

ZONES 4–8
HABIT AND SIZE Acaulis type. Clump forming. Stem height 4 in. (10 cm).
FLOWERING Late winter to midspring.
CULTIVATION Acaulis primroses appreciate a mulch to retain soil moisture.
ORIGIN A Barnhaven seed strain produced by Florence Bellis.
LANDSCAPE AND DESIGN USES They work very well in combination with other acaulis primroses. White spring flowers such as *Leucojum* (spring snowflakes), *Galanthus* (snowdrops), or white *Muscari* (grape hyacinth) will offset the pastel blues. They grow well in containers and look lovely in white ceramic pots. We often display them in baskets with white crocuses.
SIMILAR PLANTS You will find many blue acaulis on the market, such as *P.* 'True Blue', a hybrid of *P. vulgaris* in shades of bright blue.

Primula Candy Pinks Group

This is a pink strain of the low-growing primrose. It comes in several shades of true, clear pink—bright satin pink, soft peach, shell, salmon, and baby pink. It flowers profusely, and for every flower picked another will appear. All have yellow centres.

ZONES 4–8
HABIT AND SIZE Acaulis type. Clump forming. Stem height 4 in. (10 cm).
FLOWERING Late winter to midspring.
ORIGIN A Barnhaven seed strain produced by Florence Bellis.
LANDSCAPE AND DESIGN USES As is true for most of the other acaulis plants, we love the pink shades in containers or planted with other pastel colours and with some dark pink heathers. Try white hellebores underplanted with a carpet of pink primroses.
SIMILAR PLANTS *Primula acaulis* Danova Series Rose Improved and Pink Improved series have flowers with a large yellow centre; the bloom is somewhat frillier and the foliage is a darker green. *Primula vulgaris* Dobra Group has large, dark pink flowers. *Primula vulgaris* subsp. *sibthorpii* is native to eastern Europe and has rose-pink-coloured flowers with a yellow eye.

Primula Chartreuse Group

A descendant of the nineteenth century "bunch-flowered" primroses, this creamy white polyanthus has an old-fashioned feel to it and is an excellent candidate for flower arranging. It has a greeny-lime centre and large slightly ruffled flowers.

ZONES 4–8
HABIT AND SIZE Polyanthus type. Clump forming. Stem height 8 in. (20 cm).
FLOWERING Mid to late spring.
ORIGIN A Barnhaven seed strain.
LANDSCAPE AND DESIGN USES The creamy colours lend themselves to some lovely fresh combinations with green foliage plants as a backdrop. We particularly like planting them with the deep blue grape hyacinth (*Muscari armeniacum*) as a contrast; both plants grow to a similar height and flower at a similar time.
SIMILAR PLANTS *Primula* 'Stella Banana Cream' is another creamy polyanthus on the market that has more of a yellow eye.

Primula Cowichan Blue Group

We think this is one of the loveliest blues in the polyanthus form. As a Cowichan type it has the dark bronze foliage and flowers that are solid pools of intense blues, some with a black bee centre. The absence of the usual large yellow eye is the reason for the pure colour effect.

ZONES 4–8
HABIT AND SIZE Polyanthus type. Clump forming. Stem height 8 in. (20 cm).
FLOWERING Late winter to midspring.
ORIGIN This is another strain developed by Florence Bellis.
LANDSCAPE AND DESIGN USES Blues have a lovely calming effect and, as there are not many other flowers out at this time of year with this kind of hue, it will stand out beautifully in the spring garden and can be combined with many other colours. We just love it with early flowering yellow or white narcissus. In the photo, blue and yellow cowichans are planted with red tulips and ferns in a zinc container.
SIMILAR PLANTS Many other blue polyanthus are on the market. *Primula* Marine Blues Group has flowers in different shades from pale to dark blue, some with a white edge and with the usual yellow eye. *Primula* 'Crescendo Blue Shades' has uniform dark blue-purple flowers. It is a good standard polyanthus.

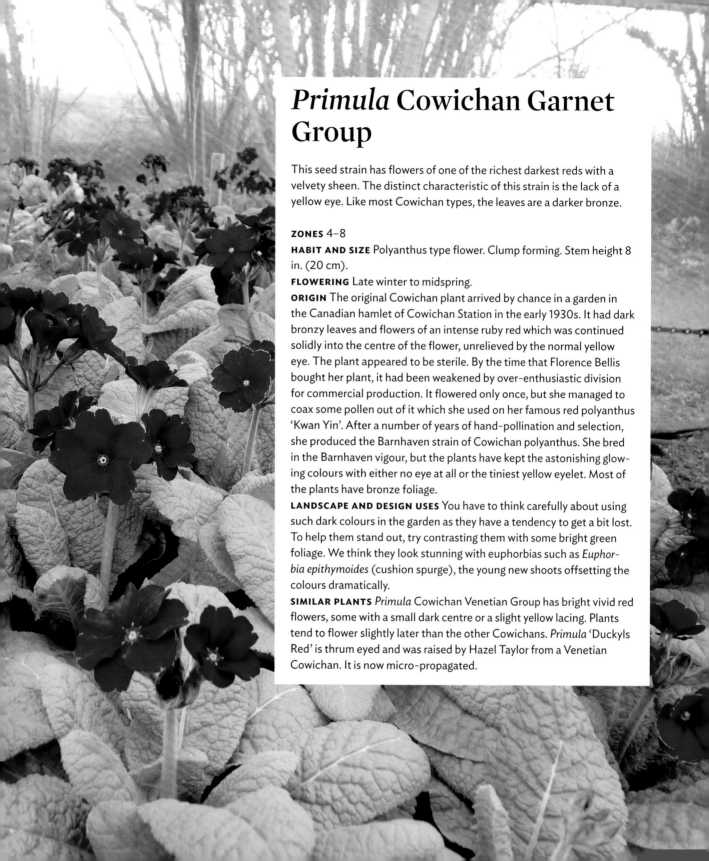

Primula Cowichan Garnet Group

This seed strain has flowers of one of the richest darkest reds with a velvety sheen. The distinct characteristic of this strain is the lack of a yellow eye. Like most Cowichan types, the leaves are a darker bronze.

ZONES 4–8

HABIT AND SIZE Polyanthus type flower. Clump forming. Stem height 8 in. (20 cm).

FLOWERING Late winter to midspring.

ORIGIN The original Cowichan plant arrived by chance in a garden in the Canadian hamlet of Cowichan Station in the early 1930s. It had dark bronzy leaves and flowers of an intense ruby red which was continued solidly into the centre of the flower, unrelieved by the normal yellow eye. The plant appeared to be sterile. By the time that Florence Bellis bought her plant, it had been weakened by over-enthusiastic division for commercial production. It flowered only once, but she managed to coax some pollen out of it which she used on her famous red polyanthus 'Kwan Yin'. After a number of years of hand-pollination and selection, she produced the Barnhaven strain of Cowichan polyanthus. She bred in the Barnhaven vigour, but the plants have kept the astonishing glowing colours with either no eye at all or the tiniest yellow eyelet. Most of the plants have bronze foliage.

LANDSCAPE AND DESIGN USES You have to think carefully about using such dark colours in the garden as they have a tendency to get a bit lost. To help them stand out, try contrasting them with some bright green foliage. We think they look stunning with euphorbias such as *Euphorbia epithymoides* (cushion spurge), the young new shoots offsetting the colours dramatically.

SIMILAR PLANTS *Primula* Cowichan Venetian Group has bright vivid red flowers, some with a small dark centre or a slight yellow lacing. Plants tend to flower slightly later than the other Cowichans. *Primula* 'Duckyls Red' is thrum eyed and was raised by Hazel Taylor from a Venetian Cowichan. It is now micro-propagated.

Primula Crescendo Golden Group

This strain of commercial polyanthus has stood the test of time as very uniform, hardy hybrids. The plants have large, very vivid uniform colours and strong stems, and they flower reliably when they should. This particular series has deep orange-yellow flowers and is widely available as plug plants and seeds. Though often grown as annuals, they are really perennials when grown in the right conditions.

ZONES 4–8
HABIT AND SIZE Polyanthus form. Forms clumps of 6–10 in. (15–25 cm). Stem height 8 in. (20 cm).
FLOWERING Late winter to early spring.
ORIGIN The various Crescendo strains originated from Ernst Benary Seed Growers, a German plant-breeding company that has been in existence since 1843. K. Wagner was responsible for bringing the Crescendo strains onto the market along with many other series such as *P.* Joker.
LANDSCAPE AND DESIGN USES These polyanthus have good consistent shape and form and their bright colours lend themselves well to formal displays or large bedding displays with tulips or pansies. This is a good strain to choose when looking for uniform mass planting schemes. You will often see them in local authority plantings.
SIMILAR PLANTS *Primula* Crescendo Series is available in white, gold, blue, red, or pink. *Primula* Rainbow Series, a polyanthus form trialled by the Royal Horticultural Society, are hardy plants with consistent flowering and scented flowers; they come in a range of colours—Golden, Blue, Bright Red, and Scarlet Cream. The series was raised and introduced by Floranova in England.

Primula 'Dark Rosaleen'

'Dark Rosaleen' is a lovely hybrid. It has dark green leaves with an unusual bronze red sheen to them. The flowers are quite striking and are a deep red with pink stripes and a neat yellow centre. The plant has proved to be a very vigorous grower that clumps up readily and is easy to divide.

ZONES 4–9

HABIT AND SIZE Small polyanthus form. Quite compact plant. Stem height 5 in. (12 cm).

FLOWERING Early to late spring.

ORIGIN This is one of Joe Kennedy's primroses from Ireland. An avid plant breeder, he collected many of the old Irish varieties growing in various gardens and produced some beautiful hybrids. This plant is named after the poem "Dark Rosaleen" by Irish poet James Clarence Mangan. It is now widely available as a micro-propagated plant.

LANDSCAPE AND DESIGN USES Great as container plants because of their dark leaves, but they also look striking as border plants.

Primula Daybreak Group ▲

This is one of the longest flowering polyanthus we grow. In fact, it hardly ever stops flowering. After a short break in the summer, it often flowers most of the winter. The colours can be described as opalescent mother of pearl and dark-stemmed whites, often flushed or veined with apricot or rose pink, a good contrast to the bronzed foliage. Like most polyanthus blooms, they are deliciously scented.

ZONES 4–8
HABIT AND SIZE Polyanthus type. Clump forming. Stem height 8 in. (20 cm).
FLOWERING Late winter to midspring and often in autumn.
ORIGIN A Barnhaven strain introduced by Jared Sinclair.
LANDSCAPE AND DESIGN USES This is a lovely plant to brighten up a shady corner and will work well even in a small garden. However, it is also lovely on its own in a container or basket and placed in a prominent place on a terrace or balcony.
SIMILAR PLANTS *Primula* New Pinks Group has polyanthus form flowers in more uniform shades of light to dark pink. This group originated from the first true pink polyanthus which appeared in Linda Eickman's garden in Dayton, Oregon, in the early 1940s. Linda brought two plants with her in a wicker basket on a 100-mile (160-km) bus trip to Gresham to ask Florence Bellis what to do with them. Florence advised her to cross-pollinate them. Florence also used some of the pollen on her own more robust lavender-pinks, first offering the New Pinks strain for sale in 1958.

Primula Drumcliff ▼

SYNONYM *Primula vulgaris* 'K74'

This is a lovely cultivar with pink-cream flowers and striking purplish bronze leaves. Named after the resting place of W. B. Yeats.

ZONES 4–9
HABIT AND SIZE Acaulis form. Stem height 5 in. (12 cm).
FLOWERING Early to late spring.
ORIGIN This is part of a unique collection of primroses bred over 35 years from old Irish varieties by one of Ireland's amateur primrose breeders, Joe Kennedy, which was released by FitzGerald Nurseries onto the market in 2011. They are now widely available as they are being produced via micro-propagation. However, unlike many commercial primroses they have retained their hardiness and have some wonderful colours.
LANDSCAPE AND DESIGN USES Borders and containers.
SIMILAR PLANTS *Primula* Avondale 'K29' is a hybrid by Joe Kennedy with soft pink flowers, a neat ochre and yellow eye, and a streak of white running thorough each lobe of the flower. The habit is more juliana-like with a creeping rootstock.

Primula 'Francisca'

'Francisca' has very distinctive ruffled green flowers with a pale yellow eye. The flowers last up to three weeks in a vase; however, they are not scented like those of many other hybrids. Love it or hate it, this primrose will certainly be a talking point.

ZONES 4–8

HABIT AND SIZE Polyanthus type. Stem height 8 in. (20 cm).

FLOWERING Late spring and often re-flowers in the autumn.

ORIGIN The story goes that it was spotted on a traffic island in Surrey, British Columbia, by Francisca Darts, a Canadian gardener. It is probably a woodland primrose that had hybridized with a showy bedding primula. Now widely available as plug plants. The name is sometimes mispelled as "Francesca."

LANDSCAPE AND DESIGN USES An unusual addition to your primula collection in the garden or a conversation piece in a pot. The green flowers can be a useful addition to a spring border and planted in combination with a red or yellow polyanthus and Gold-laced will create an inspiring display.

SIMILAR PLANTS *Primula* 'Green Lace' bred by Sandra Tuffin from Uncommon Ground Nursery in Ontario and introduced into the trade in 2002.

Primula Gold-laced Group

Victorian gold-laced primrose
SYNONYM *Primula elatior* Victoriana Gold-laced

One of the most distinctive polyanthus primulas. With its gold-edging and dark or bright red background, it is a stunning plant. The lacing looks like it was painted on by fairy hands and creates the illusion that there are twice as many petals as there really are. A good specimen should have flat flowers with very even, neat edging and a very round centre.

ZONES 5–8
HABIT AND SIZE Spread about 8 in. (20 cm). Stem height 8 in. (20 cm).
FLOWERING Late winter to midspring.
CULTIVATION Despite its unusual appearance it is as hardy and as easy to grow as any other primrose. It does, however, seem to be an especially greedy plant, and it is worth while dividing it regularly as otherwise it tends to dwindle away.
ORIGIN A real old-fashioned primrose, the Gold-laced polyanthus was at its peak in the early nineteenth century, hence often known as the Victorian primrose. It was deemed one of the only primulas apart from auriculas worthy of being placed among the florists' flowers along with roses and pinks. Florists' feasts and shows were held and the winner was awarded a copper kettle. Some very strict criteria were laid down for judging plants at shows which are still followed to some extent in the auricula and primula societies in the United Kingdom and the United States. They are still our guidelines when selecting plants for pollinating. After the Industrial Revolution, interest in Gold-laced polyanthus declined, though a few people still grew it in small numbers, notably the members of the primula societies in England. It nearly

disappeared completely in the Second World War when a bomb hit one of the last nurseries growing them in England. The grower rescued some scraps of plants and sufficient remains were recovered to begin again. Some seed was obtained by a certain Mr Briggs who sent some to Florence Bellis, who along with a few other individual enthusiasts in the United Kingdom kept them going. More recently they have been micro-propagated with varying degrees of success and are more readily available, although the flowers are not always up to the exacting standards of the primula societies.

LANDSCAPE AND DESIGN USES While Gold-laced polyanthus do work well in the garden, it is not always easy to combine their unusual colours with other plants. A yellow daffodil such as *Narcissus* 'Tête-à-Tête' will offset the yellow lacing. However, the Gold-laced polyanthus look wonderful by themselves in containers as they are showy plants. They will make a fantastic table piece for an outside eating area or in a pot by the front door. They also look great as cut flowers and were once used as flowers for button-holes in the 1950s as they were said to work wonders with a brown suit.

SIMILAR PLANTS Several other varieties have similar features with gold or silver lacing. The Gold-Laced Group Beeches strain ▲ has a dark-red background. It is possible to find silver-laced varieties with a black background and some with purple, pink, or even blue backgrounds that would make purists throw their hands up in horror, although some of these plants are quite pretty.

Primula Harbinger Group

A white form of the wild yellow-flowered *P. vulgaris*. It has the same simple charm as the common primrose, and the pure white flowers with their yellow centres contrast beautifully with the crisp green foliage.

ZONES 4–8

HABIT AND SIZE Acaulis type. Makes very large clumps. Stem height 4 in. (10 cm).

FLOWERING Late winter to midspring.

ORIGIN This plant was originally found more than 100 years ago as a sport in a Cornish wood. It was awarded a First Class Certificate by the Royal Horticultural Society in 1882.

LANDSCAPE AND DESIGN USES We love this white simple primrose as it will go with almost anything and shows up so well in a dark corner. Contrast with some dark red polyanthus and you can't go wrong.

SIMILAR PLANTS *Primula* 'Gigha', another white vulgaris type, is originally from the Isle of Gigha off the west coast of Scotland.

Primula Indian Reds Group

This is a sturdy polyanthus in colours of scarlet and bright crimson reds.

ZONES 4–8
HABIT AND SIZE Polyanthus type. Clump forming. Stem height 8 in. (20 cm).
FLOWERING Mid to late spring.
ORIGIN A Barnhaven seed strain. It is considered one of the original Silver Dollar strains introduced by Florence Bellis. The flowers were said to be the size of a silver dollar. Many of the names of the original series betray their American origins, such as 'Grand Canyon' or 'Desert Sunset'.
LANDSCAPE AND DESIGN USES Borders or container planting. Wonderful with yellow tulips such as *Tulipa* 'Mrs John T. Scheepers'.
SIMILAR PLANTS *Primula* Little Egypt Group is an elegant, dark-stemmed strain with vivid colours in red, orange, and pyramid brick shades. *Primula* Ramona Group has flowers that are more coppery red.

Primula Innisfree

SYNONYM *Primula vulgaris* 'K72'

A very deep red velvety flower with a yellow centre over dark green foliage. It also has a fairly long flowering period. Named after the famous poem by W. B. Yeats called "The Lake Isle of Innisfree."

ZONES 4–9

HABIT AND SIZE Acaulis form. Quite compact plants that divide easily. Stem height 6 in. (15 cm).

FLOWERING Early to late spring.

ORIGIN Another of the Kennedy Irish primroses released in 2011 and marketed by FitzGerald Nurseries.

LANDSCAPE AND DESIGN USES Great as a container plant because of its dark leaves but it also looks striking in the border.

Primula Midnight Group

These rich luscious velvety blooms come in shades of deep blue-blacks and magenta-purples. Some have white centres and some are edged with silver wire.

ZONES 4–8
HABIT AND SIZE Polyanthus type. Clump forming. Stem height 8 in. (20 cm).
FLOWERING Late winter to midspring.
ORIGIN A Barnhaven seed strain introduced by the Sinclairs in the United Kingdom. It appeared as a natural break in the Mauve Victorian strain and was then line-bred to separate out a new darker strain.
LANDSCAPE AND DESIGN USES Although these are fairly dark flowers and not always easy to place in the garden, we think that as long as they are contrasted with light-coloured flowers such as *Primula* 'Sorbet', they are really magical. We often grow them in containers with white *Narcissus* 'Paper White'.

Primula Spice Shades Group

Usually when one thinks of brown, a drab colour comes to mind. This vibrant strain is far from dull however and displays a wide variation of unusual shades of chocolate, coffee, cinnamon, allspice, ginger and hazelnut browns, with the occasional yellow. Fragrant as spices, too, are these Spice Polyanthus, for you will notice that the colours having yellow as a predominant ancestor are apt to carry some of the cowslip perfume in varying degrees of deliciousness.

ZONES 4–8
HABIT AND SIZE Polyanthus type. Clump forming. Stem height 8 in. (20 cm).
FLOWERING Late winter to midspring.
ORIGIN A Barnhaven strain born in 1953
LANDSCAPE AND DESIGN USES An unusual rich colour range which works well with other yellow primroses, yellow pansies, or perhaps in a basket with yellow-and-white *Narcissus* 'Jenny' for a lovely old-fashioned look.
SIMILAR PLANTS *Primula* 'Gilded Ginger' has similar tones of bitter chocolate but with a large yellow gold centre and often a yellow edge. *Primula* 'Firecracker', a polyanthus form with a yellow-gold centre and orangey red tones at the edges, is relatively new on the market and may need some protection from frost.

Primula Winter White Group ▼

Large white blooms with a yellow centre. The plants produce many flowers on strong stems. Sweetly scented.

ZONES 4–8
HABIT AND SIZE Polyanthus form. Clump forming. Stem height 8 in. (20 cm).
FLOWERING Late winter to midspring.
ORIGIN This is the direct descendant of Gertrude Jeckyll's Munstead strain developed in the 1880s. It took Miss Jeckyll some ten to fifteen years to produce a fairly large flowering strain of white, yellow, and orange polyanthus from two small-flowered plants she found in cottagers' gardens. In fact, most of today's polyanthus forms stem from the first "modern" polyanthus raised in her garden at Munstead. Barnhaven continued her work on these original strains without adding any other genes to the mix. *Primula* Harvest Yellows Group also stems from the original Munstead strains.
LANDSCAPE AND DESIGN USES White polyanthus play an important role in many of our displays. The white stands out beautifully in the garden and can be used to offset nearly every colour in the spectrum. When used to brighten up a dark corner, they work especially well in combination with bright yellow polyanthus, yellow daffodils, and Bowles' golden grass to add some bright green foliage. And for those of you looking for some early colour in an all-white garden, they are a very useful player.
SIMILAR PLANTS Many other white polyanthus are on the market, including *P.* Crescendo White Group and *P.* 'Stella Snow White'.

Primula Striped Victorians Group ▲

This is a real showstopper. The flowers are striped like Japanese irises. The blooms are fairly large with a yellow centre and can have blue or mauve stripes. There is a fair amount of variation in this seed strain.

ZONES 4–8
HABIT AND SIZE Polyanthus type. Clump forming. Stem height 8 in. (20 cm).
FLOWERING Late winter to midspring.
ORIGIN This strain harks back to the 1950s and was first introduced by Florence Bellis.
LANDSCAPE AND DESIGN USES With such exceptionally attractive blooms, Striped Victorians are great at eye level on their own in containers that can be placed in a prominent position by a front door. They will also look good as border plants in a small garden.
SIMILAR PLANTS *Primula* 'Zebra Blue' is a striped acaulis recently launched on the market, developed by Stijn van Hoecke in Belgium, and is widely available as a plug plant or as seed. It is a compact plant with larger, very bright blooms. There will also be some variation in the flowers. *Primula* 'Tie Dye' is a similar colour though the veined markings aren't as pronounced and it is also slightly less hardy. Height 4–5 in. (10–12 cm).

DOUBLE PRIMROSES

Often more than 100 blooms on a single small plant—that's a double primrose. They have existed for centuries, and from time to time occur naturally without human intervention. In the past, they were dug up where they were found and cosseted, named, and divided. A modern example is 'Sue Jervis', which was introduced in 1980 and is said to have been found growing wild in Shropshire, England. As far back as 1597, double primroses are mentioned in literature such as in John Gerard's *Herbal*, where the text talks about "Our Garden Double primrose." John Parkinson in 1629 wrote of "the ordinary double primrose" as if it was very common indeed.

Creating new plants, however, is an altogether different matter, because double primroses don't carry seed. When a promising new double appears, it can only be reproduced by division or by micropropagation. This is the reason for the limited number of double varieties on the market. Many of them have been around for many years and many of the old varieties have disappeared. Some of the big plant-propagating companies are now taking an interest in double primroses again, and some new exciting plants are appearing on the market with the promise of more to come, so watch this space. We make no apologies for including some older varieties in our recommendations. There is room for recent introductions with their neat habits, but also for the slightly unruly look of the old-fashioned kind.

Try planting double primroses under small shrubs, such as *Acer* (maple), rose bushes, or even gooseberry bushes in the vegetable garden. They will then be protected from the sun later in the year when the shrubs are in full leaf. Use them to complement other plants—double white primroses under dark slate-coloured hellebores, for instance, look very classy. We love planting them in old-fashioned baskets and in large pots with small grasses or ivy, to have them close at hand.

Primula Belarina Cream

SYNONYM *Primula* 'Kerbelcrem'

An outstanding double primrose with large cream flowers and fresh green foliage. This is one of nine colours presently listed from this stable. It produces vigorous plants that divide well and, as with most doubles, is incredibly floriferous. In contrast to some other plants on the market, it has fully double flowers, that is, the flowers stay double when they are fully open. The plant has strong flower stems and upright-facing blooms.

ZONES 4–8

HABIT AND SIZE Acaulis type. Forming clumps of 6–8 in. (15–20 cm). Stem height 4–6 in. (10–15 cm).

FLOWERING Early to late spring.

ORIGIN All of the Belarina double primrose cultivars arose from crosses made by David and Priscilla Kerley in the United Kingdom. First introduced in 2004, the plants quickly became popular with gardeners on both sides of the Atlantic. The Kerleys are currently working on extending their colour range and hope to introduce some interesting purple-edged doubles and light blues in the future.

LANDSCAPE AND DESIGN USES Containers and edging. They are offset nicely by green foliage plants such as ferns.

SIMILAR PLANTS Belarina Buttermilk is a pale yellow double primrose from the same source but in rosette form—the flowers surrounded by green, otherwise known as Jack-in-the-Green.

Primula Belarina Valentine

SYNONYM *Primula* 'Kerbelred'

A vibrant red double primrose plant with a compact shape and upright-facing blooms. Vigorous and bears a huge number of flowers, which are fully double, remaining so for the flowering period.

ZONES 4–8
HABIT AND SIZE Acaulis type. Form clumps of 6–8 in. (15–20 cm). Stem height 4–6 in. (10–15 cm).
FLOWERING Early to late spring.
ORIGIN Raised by David and Priscilla Kerley in England.
LANDSCAPE AND DESIGN USES Containers and edging.
SIMILAR PLANTS 'Corporal Baxter' double primrose, bred by Jared Sinclair, is an old faithful and easy to grow. It is not such a tidy plant as some of the modern doubles, but perhaps more true to type, being a little undisciplined. 'April Rose' double primrose was originally raised from Barnhaven seed and described as a rich dark pink. Tissue-cultured plants are readily available in North America, though some of them have garnet red flowers, raising doubts as to whether this is still the original plant.

Primula 'Blue Ice'

Prolific pale powder blue flowers, with a fresh light green foliage. Quite early flowering compared to some of the other doubles, it produces an abundance of flowers on strong stems and has a long flowering period.

ZONES 4–8
HABIT AND SIZE Acaulis type. Forms large clumps of 6–8 in. (15–20 cm). Stem height 4–6 in. (10–15 cm).
FLOWERING Early winter to midspring.
ORIGIN A Barnhaven double introduced in 2014 by Lynne who has a passion for pale blues and has worked on them extensively for a number of years.
LANDSCAPE AND DESIGN USES Simply lovely on their own in a container or in a border.
SIMILAR PLANTS 'Blue Sapphire' is absolutely glorious when in full flower. The plant is entirely covered with an abundance of true blue blossoms. An old faithful and very reliable, it probably appeared in the 1980s.

Primula 'Camaieu'

It's the variety of shades that we love about this one. The buds begin as a buttery yellow, then change to shaded pinks with a finale of mauve. The plant produces a veritable explosion of flowers which appear very early in the season.

ZONES 4–8

HABIT AND SIZE Acaulis form. Makes a large clump of 6–8 in. (15–20 cm). Stem height 4–6 in. (10–15 cm).

FLOWERING Late winter to midspring.

ORIGIN The seedling first flowered at Barnhaven in 2003.

LANDSCAPE AND DESIGN USES We always have a few baskets of these dotted about, but in the garden, in combination with other white doubles, you will have a very pretty display.

SIMILAR PLANTS Belarina Pink Ice double primrose has white flowers with a pink blush that matures from pink to pale purple, giving a fresh bi-coloured look. It has slightly larger flowers than 'Camaieu'. 'Pink Star' double primrose, a Barnhaven hybrid, is a true pink double, with very faintly striped petals.

Primula 'Dawn Ansell'

An impressive plant in the garden, this is a white Jack-in-the Green primrose, which means that the flowers are surrounded by a large ruff of green leaves. The fully double roselike flowers appear in late winter to add an ephemeral glow in the garden.

ZONES 4–8

HABIT AND SIZE Forms clumps 6–8 in. (15–20 cm). Stem height 4–6 in. (10–15 cm).

FLOWERING Late winter to midspring.

ORIGIN Raised from seed in the 1960s by Cecil Jones, a Welsh hybridizer of distinction. It is now widely available thanks to micro-propagation.

LANDSCAPE AND DESIGN USES Stunning in a vase and the ruffs look good for ages after the flower petals have died.

SIMILAR PLANTS Belarina Buttercup Yellow is also a Jack-in-the-Green form, but with bright yellow flowers; it was raised by David and Priscilla Kerley in England.

Primula 'Guernsey Cream'

Rich creamy coloured blooms set against very dark bronze foliage make a striking contrast. The stems are red and the leaves are veined with red. This vigorous grower tends to have large leaves.

ZONES 4–8

HABIT AND SIZE Acaulis form. Forms large clumps of 6–8 in. (15–20 cm). Stem height 4–6 in. (10–15 cm).

FLOWERING Early to late spring.

ORIGIN A Barnhaven double introduced in 2014. It came from an old cross between our acaulis 'Osiered Amber' and probably some pollen from a yellow double primrose.

LANDSCAPE AND DESIGN USES Try these in a container with green foliage plants such as some trailing variegated ivy for a classy display.

Primula 'Ken Dearman'

A lovely double with flowers in shades of copper, burnt orange, and yellow.

ZONES 4–8
HABIT AND SIZE An acaulis type double primrose. Makes clumps of 6–8 in. (15–20 cm). Stem height 4–6 in. (10–15 cm).
FLOWERING Late winter to midspring.
ORIGIN A Barnhaven introduction that has been micro-propagated and is widely available.
LANDSCAPE AND DESIGN USES A good container plant or used as edging in a border.
SIMILAR PLANTS Belarina Nectarine double primrose is a Jack-in-the-Green or rosette double primrose in yellow and orange blushed with pink. 'Pink Grapefruit' double primrose is slightly later to flower than some doubles, an absolute riot of peach and yellow shades. It flowers like there's no tomorrow.

Primula 'Lilacina Plena'

Double lilac primrose
SYNONYM *Primula vulgaris* 'Quaker's Bonnet'

A classic, old-fashioned double primrose. This, or something similar, is the one folks say their grandmother had in the garden. Prolific pale lilac blooms, slightly unruly, but that's part of the joy of it. An easy plant to cultivate and divide.

ZONES 4–8

HABIT AND SIZE Forms clumps of 6–8 in. (15–20 cm). Stem height 4–6 in. (10–15 cm).

FLOWERING Early to late spring.

ORIGIN A very old variety—some say hundreds of years.

LANDSCAPE AND DESIGN USES A great garden plant that will form good clumps in any shady spot.

SIMILAR PLANTS *Primula* 'Marie Crousse', an old double primrose, possibly of French origin, has lilac flowers speckled with white, with some short polyanthus forms. The plant is very vigorous and easy but it is getting harder to obtain. *Primula* 'Lilian Harvey' is a cerise pink double primrose from Barnhaven that has been micro-propagated.

Primula 'Miss Indigo'

A deservedly well-known double with silver lacing on almost navy blue to violet flowers. Widely available and easy to grow. A neat plant with a heady abundance of stems coming from the centre.

ZONES 4–8

HABIT AND SIZE Acaulis type. Forms clumps of 6–8 in. (15–20 cm). Stem height 4–6 in. (10–15 cm).

FLOWERING Late winter to midspring.

ORIGIN Bred by Jared Sinclair of Barnhaven and one of the most widely grown Barnhaven doubles.

LANDSCAPE AND DESIGN USES Great in containers with other double primroses or in a shady border with some white wood anemone.

SIMILAR PLANTS 'Granny Graham' double primrose, described as "the violet blue of a summer midnight," seems to be mainly available in the United States. 'Eugenie' double primrose, from Barnhaven, has paler violet-blue flowers with a lovely white edge.

Primula 'Petticoat'

The feature that stands out is the whiteness of the flowers. They are paper white, contrasted with a good fresh green leaf. A refreshing plant, beautiful in bud and in flower, and one of the earliest to bloom in spring.

ZONES 4–8
HABIT AND SIZE Forms clumps of 6–8 in. (15–20 cm). Stem height 4 in. (10 cm).
FLOWERING Late winter to early spring.
CULTIVATION One of the easier plants to divide.
ORIGIN The origins of this cultivar have been difficult to trace, but it has been micropropagated in the United Kingdom since the 1990s.
LANDSCAPE AND DESIGN USES This looks lovely in a zinc container or basket. Contrast with 'Miss Indigo' or 'Lilacina Plena'.
SIMILAR PLANTS 'Alba Plena', a white double primrose, dating from the dark ages, is known in North America as 'Cottage White' or 'Double White'. It has long, somewhat straggly stalks but is very vigorous and free flowering.

Primula 'Sunshine Susie'

This is another old double that has stood the test of time. It has masses of golden yellow flowers with an occasional pink tinge to the edges of the petals. The habit is somewhat untidy, but the plant is a lovely vigorous addition to any border.

ZONES 4–8

HABIT AND SIZE Forms clumps of 6–8 in. (15–20 cm). Stem height 4 in. (10 cm).

FLOWERING Early to late spring.

ORIGIN A Barnhaven introduction

LANDSCAPE AND DESIGN USES Great edging plant. Offset it with some green foliage such as heucheras.

SIMILAR PLANTS Belarina Yellow Ruffle double primrose has very large bright cheerful yellow flowers on a very compact plant. The long-lasting flowers have the added bonus of being fragrant like most of the yellows.

Primula 'Val Horncastle'

An attractive pure pale yellow double with fresh green foliage. Large very double flowers.

ZONES 4–8

HABIT AND SIZE Acaulis type. Forms clumps of 6–8 in. (15–20 cm). Stem height 4–6 in. (10–15 cm).

FLOWERING Early to late spring.

ORIGIN Another Barnhaven double from the group produced in the late 1960s and popular ever since.

LANDSCAPE AND DESIGN USES Containers or border.

JULIANA PRIMULAS

Listed in commercial catalogues as Wandas, Julianas, or Pruhonicians, these primulas are all hybrids of *P. juliae*. The original *P. juliae* was discovered in the Caucasus at the beginning of the twentieth century. A tiny plant with bright magenta flowers, it also had a very different vigorous growing habit to the other species of European wild primroses. Its creeping (or stoloniferous) rootstock meant that it spread easily and lent itself particularly well to division. It also had an earlier flowering period. This explains the excitement on its discovery and why it has been used in breeding large numbers of hybrids that we see today.

Because they are petite plants, julianas merit being used where they can be easily seen. They are great for window boxes and pots on the front doorstep, and combine well with snowdrops, scillas, crocuses, and small daffodils, as they bloom around the same time. Julianas do really well in rockeries, generously spreading themselves and providing easy, long-lasting colour. With their short, tufted habit, they provide useful ground cover. If planted alongside other polyanthus primulas, they will provide early colour before the main display comes along.

Julianas are generally small-flowered, but make up in exuberance what they lack in size. When conditions suit them, they provide a mound of flowers, with hardly a leaf visible, for a full three months. They are vigorous, fail-safe, and easy to grow. Their creeping rootstock means they will spread faster than many of the clump-forming polyanthus and primroses. They often have rounder leaves, which can be quite dark or striking in colour and contrast well with the flowers.

Primula Blue Juliana Group

Blue Julies, Blue julianas

This must be one of our favourites simply because of its very early and long flowering period. Flower colour in this strain varies widely from light blue to a dark purple-blue. Some flowers have a red ring or star around the yellow eye. At the height of flowering, you will hardly be able to see the leaves under the profusion of flowers.

ZONES 4–9
HABIT AND SIZE Acaulis type. Forms clumps which spread readily and are easy to divide. Stem height 3 in. (8 cm).
FLOWERING Late winter to midspring.
ORIGIN A Barnhaven seed strain.
LANDSCAPE AND DESIGN USES This juliana can be used to carpet under trees or line a northern wall. It is best grown in large clumps.
SIMILAR PLANTS You can sometimes find *P.* 'Blue Riband', which strongly resembles a blue juliana, at specialist nurseries. It was raised in Scotland by George Murray and has deep green leaves with amethyst-blue flowers. The small yellow eye is ringed with crimson, making it easily identifiable.

Primula Fireflies Group

This red-flowered polyanthus type juliana has the characteristic small flowers and dark leaves. The flowers are a dark, luscious red with hardly any or no yellow eye, reminiscent of the various Cowichan groups.

ZONES 4–8
HABIT AND SIZE Polyanthus type. Clump forming. Stem height 5 in. (12 cm).
FLOWERING Late winter to midspring.
ORIGIN A Barnhaven seed strain dating back to Florence Bellis.
LANDSCAPE AND DESIGN USES Great in containers with *Euphorbia* Redwing 'Charam' or in the garden with a spread of yellow winter aconites.

Primula Footlight Parade Group

This bewitching strain of juliana hybrids comes in shades of clear pink, smoked salmon, burnt orange, pastel orange, maraschino, raspberry, coral, salmon, peach, apricot, orange-red, and citron yellow.

ZONES 4–9

HABIT AND SIZE Polyanthus type, but shorter than the majority. Stem height 5 in. (12 cm).

FLOWERING Late winter to midspring.

ORIGIN A Barnhaven seed strain, one of the original Florence Bellis creations.

LANDSCAPE AND DESIGN USES The really bright colours of this group work well at the front of a border, especially as the plants are much lower growing polyanthus than many others. We like it with sedges such as *Carex comans* bronze-leaved. It is also good for containers where the small neat flowers can be appreciated.

SIMILAR PLANTS *Primula* 'Don Keefe' has orange-red flowers and was raised from Barnhaven seed and propagated by Bob Brown of Cotswold Garden Flowers in England.

Primula 'Guinevere'

SYNONYM *Primula* 'Garryard Guinevere'

This magical variety simply shimmers in the garden. The leaves are purplish bronze and the umbels carry purplish pink, yellow-eyed flowers on red stems.

ZONES 3–8

HABIT AND SIZE Polyanthus type. Creeping rootstock. Stem height 4 in. (12 cm).

FLOWERING Late winter to midspring.

ORIGIN A very old Irish variety. The name comes from Garryard House near Naas in County Kildaire and originates from a cross between *P. juliae* and *P. vulgaris*. Although the origins of the plant are slightly obscure, Cecil Monson, a primrose breeder, records the plant growing in a garden in 1935 and attributes it to a Mrs Johnson of Kinlough.

LANDSCAPE AND DESIGN USES We love combining this plant in a container with the dramatic purple foliage of heucheras, such as *Heuchera* 'Spellbound', to offset the pink flowers wonderfully. In the garden, a spread of 'Garryard Guinevere' contrasting with the Japanese painted fern *Athyrium niponicum* 'Pictum' would be superb.

SIMILAR PLANTS Many other primroses have "Garryard" in their name, but this seems to be attributed to any dark-leaved variety even though there is no necessary connection to 'Guinevere' parentage. The only other well-documented 'Garryard' primrose is 'Garryard Appleblossom' with white-and-pink blooms, though it is rarely offered for sale and is said to date back to the 1800s. *Primula* 'Avoca' has similar dark chocolate foliage with a purple tone and light pink-purple flowers.

Primula 'Jay-Jay'

SYNONYM *Primula* ×*pruhonica* 'Jay-Jay'

One of the most intensely coloured juliana type primroses, 'Jay-Jay' has a very bright magenta flower with a small yellow centre. It is a Jack-in the-Green form, which means it has a green ruff around the flowers. It is considered to be one of the most reliable and prolific primroses in the Pacific Northwest. It also has dark green crinkled foliage.

ZONES 4–8
HABIT AND SIZE Forms low-lying clumps and spreads rapidly by rhizomes. Stem height 5 in. (12 cm).
FLOWERING Early spring.
ORIGIN This American hybrid was raised from seed labelled "*juliae* × Jack" found among some seed left after the death in 1957 of Peter Klein, a keen member of the American Primrose Society from Tacoma who bred many double primroses.
LANDSCAPE AND DESIGN USES Useful for covering large areas quickly, this primrose has a very vivid magenta colour, so place it where it will complement surrounding plants and not clash. Great on rockeries when given some shade from afternoon sun.
SIMILAR PLANTS Other similar juliana hybrids include *P.* 'Tawny Port' or *P.* 'Old Port', both with darker flowers.

Primula 'Kinlough Beauty'

Salmon-pink flowers that usually have a characteristic cream stripe down each petal. Light green roundish leaves. This is one of the most distinctive and popular juliana hybrids.

ZONES 4–9
HABIT AND SIZE Miniature polyanthus. Creeping root-stock. Stem height 3 in. (8 cm).
FLOWERING Early to midspring.
ORIGIN Kinlough, county Leitrim, Ireland.
LANDSCAPE AND DESIGN USES A delicate plant that looks lovely grown in large clumps.
SIMILAR PLANTS *Primula* 'Carrigdale', a Kennedy primrose, has a white flower that picks up pink tinges as it matures. *Primula* 'Tatyana' has similar small polyanthus flowers in brilliant pink with a white petal stripe.

Primula 'Lady Greer'

This quietly unassuming plant has small bottle green foliage and creamy yellow flowers. When grown in a pot it can seem quite ordinary, but in the garden it really comes into its own, producing masses of flower stems and spreading rapidly into large clumps. The flowers have the added bonus of being fragrant.

ZONES 3–9
HABIT AND SIZE Miniature polyanthus type. Creeping habit. Stem height 5 in. (12 cm).
FLOWERING Late winter to early spring.
ORIGIN Another plant of Irish origin that was grown by Mrs Johnson of Kinlough at the beginning of the twentieth century.
LANDSCAPE AND DESIGN USES In a woodland setting 'Lady Greer' can literally light up a dark area. It is also lovely as edging in a border.
SIMILAR PLANTS *Primula* 'Dorothy' is a miniature polyanthus with slightly larger flowers and more of a pink tinge to them, but it also has bottle green foliage and fluted flowers. It is commonly grown in British Columbia and Alaska though it is difficult to say where it originated.

Primula 'Schneekissen'

SYNONYMS *Primula* Snowcushion, *P. juliae* 'Alba'

There is a lot of confusion surrounding the name of the white juliana hybrids on the market and it is not always easy to be certain of their origins. The plants should have dainty, pure white flowers with a small yellow centre and distinctive juliana-type bright green foliage. They also should spread on creeping roots like the wild *P. juliae*. You can literally chop it into tiny bits and off it goes again.

ZONES 3–9
HABIT AND SIZE Acaulis form. Creeping rootstock. Stem height 4 in. (10 cm).
FLOWERING Late winter to midspring.
ORIGIN The original 'Schneekissen' was reportedly bred by George Arends in Germany in 1931 and has pure white pin-eyed flowers.
LANDSCAPE AND DESIGN USES Lovely at the edge of borders or rockeries, but it will also caper about under trees. A treat with *Muscari* 'Blue Star'.
SIMILAR PLANTS *Primula* 'Craddock White' is an old hybrid with large bronze-veined dark green leaves. The white flowers are slightly larger and frillier than 'Schneekissen'. *Primula* 'White Wanda' is a very similar hybrid.

Primula Vera Maud Group

This lovely juliana hybrid strain has dark red stems and flowers in delicate shell-pink shades. Many of the flowers have a darker pink edge and dark juliana-type compact leaves.

ZONES 4–8

HABIT AND SIZE Acaulis form, clump forming. Stem height 3 in. (8 cm).

FLOWERING Early spring.

ORIGIN This is a Barnhaven strain introduced in 2006. These little beauties are dear to our hearts and named after Lynne's Aunt Vera.

LANDSCAPE AND DESIGN USES Although the Vera Maud series look great in the border, their small flowers and delicate colouring merit being close to the eye to be appreciated. We grow them in shallow earthenware or zinc pots with *Cyclamen coum* that flowers at similar times.

SIMILAR PLANTS *Primula* Woodland Walk Group is a new acaulis strain bred by Vale Royal Horticultural, and it's too early to judge how the plants perform in the garden. They have similar shades of pink or white with pink tinges, some with pink edges and dark bronze foliage. Plug plants and seeds are now available.

Primula 'Wanda'

SYNONYM *Primula juliae* 'Wanda'

Many modern acaulis cultivars sold as bedding plants are called 'Wanda' or 'Wanda Mixtures', which makes it very confusing as they bear no resemblance whatsoever to the juliana hybrids. The "real" Wanda, if such a thing still exists, originated from a hybrid of *P. vulgaris* and *P. juliae* and bears masses of bright magenta flowers. It is a very easy plant to grow as it seems to thrive in most situations. Many 'Wanda' hybrids are in circulation especially in North America, maybe because they seem to cope well with higher temperatures compared to the *P. vulgaris* hybrids. 'Wanda' has bright green leaves which are slightly larger than the wild *P. juliae* but slightly rounder and glossier than the common primrose. The cultivar's main distinctive feature is its creeping habit, a characteristic of all juliana hybrids.

ZONES 3–9

HABIT AND SIZE Acaulis form. Low-growing, the plants spread by creeping rhizomes to form small clumps. Stem height 3–6 in. (8–15 cm).

FLOWERING Late winter to midspring.

ORIGIN 'Wanda' was reportedly raised by Bakers Nursery near Wolverhampton, England, around 1918 and was named after one of the director's wives. The original plant, however, probably no longer exists and today's cultivars are descendants or other hybrids.

LANDSCAPE AND DESIGN USES Lovely with some blue forget-me-nots (*Myosotis*).

SIMILAR PLANTS Some good cultivars are *P.* 'Perle von Bottrop', which has large regal purple flowers, or *P.* 'Rowena', which has pale magenta flowers.

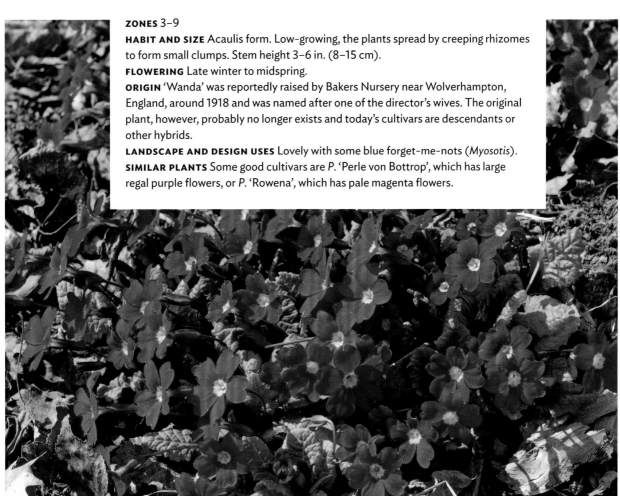

UNUSUAL FORMS

This section includes the often bizarre primulas that were much sought after in the seventeenth and eighteenth centuries known as Anomalous, Elizabethan, or Enthusiast's primroses. They still hold a fascination today, not least because they are often great garden plants. They are in fact mutations where the calyx differs from normal flowers. In the hose-in-hose forms, the calyx resembles the petals so that it appears there is one flower sitting inside another, while in the Jack-in-the-Green forms, the calyx has become leaflike and the flower nestles inside a ruff of leaves. There are many intermediate types with rather fanciful names but these two are the most readily available commercially.

The origins of this fascinating group are lost in the mists of time but the first written record seems to date from 1597. Many of the old named varieties that first appeared in Ireland and England have disappeared, but it is now possible to obtain seed and plants of these fascinating collectors' pieces from specialist nurseries. Barnhaven has been selling anomalous strains since 1949, and many other breeders such as Margaret Webster and Joe Kennedy have produced some wonderful cultivars.

Because these forms are grown for their novelty value, it obviously makes sense to locate them where they will be highly visible or in pots to make a good talking piece. For flower arrangers, it would be worth growing a patch of Jack-in-the-Greens in the cutting garden for the simple reason that they have they own inbuilt greenery—the ruff, which stays green long after the flower has faded—and they are sublime in a small posy or bouquet.

Primula Hose-in-hose Forms

Polyanthus hose-in-hose, cup and saucer primrose

In hose-in-hose flowers the calyx is transformed into petals to give the impression of one flower inside another. The name derives from the way gentlemen in Elizabethan times wore their stockings, one inside the other with the outer stocking turned down. In the garden, these forms give the impression of being particularly colourful flowery plants.

ZONES 4–8
HABIT AND SIZE Most hose-in-hose forms on the market are polyanthus type as the stalks on the acaulis forms tend not to be able to carry the extra weight of the blooms, causing them to droop, but you may find them occasionally. Stem height 8 in. (20 cm).
FLOWERING Early to midspring.
ORIGIN The hose-in-hose mutation occurs frequently in the wild and we often have plants that will naturally produce hose-in-hose forms, but Barnhaven has been

selling selected anomalous strains since 1949. They are available as unnamed plants ▲ that are divided into colour strains or as seed strains.

The You and Me Series of hose-in-hose primula ◀ is available as a seed strain and as plants. The Series is the result of years of breeding. About seven or eight colours are available, including silvery white, buttery cream, citrus yellow, warm golden yellow, rosy pink, clean red, dark purple, and even blue. Most of the flowers have golden throats, some marked with bands of red or white, and some have tidy white edging like a sliver-lace primrose.

The story of how this strain came into being is a fascinating one. Florence Bellis sent some of her hose-in-hose types to a Czech genetic researcher, Otka Placoava, who spent another 40 years to refine genetics and isolate the stable breeding lines of hose-in-hose primroses in varying colours. This was developed by one of Europe's most adventurous seed companies Sahin, to result in a dozen distinct colours of stable, fragrant hose-in-hose primroses.

LANDSCAPE AND DESIGN USES In borders or as a conversation piece in a pot. With a wide choice of colours to choose from, they are a very exciting strain to grow from seed.

Primula Lady Agatha Group

SYNONYM *Primula veris* 'Lady Agatha'

This is a yellow hose-in-hose seed strain of the cowslip with bright yellow slightly drooping flowers. We like it for its historical value as a revival of an old form first recorded in 1614 but it is also a lovely garden plant. The hose-in-hose form gives the impression of there being more flowers than there really are. It is fragrant, very hardy, and easy to grow.

ZONES 3–9

HABIT AND SIZE Cowslip form. Makes large clumps. Stem height 8 in. (20 cm).

FLOWERING Mid to late spring.

ORIGIN These exquisite flowers were first remarked upon as naturally occurring in the wild in 1614 and were much sought after in the eighteenth century. This is a Barnhaven seed strain first reintroduced in 2013.

LANDSCAPE AND DESIGN USES The tall floriferous stems really stand out in the border when grown with other spring-flowering perennials.

SIMILAR PLANTS There are other strains on the market such as the one bred by Ray Brown, owner of Plant World Seeds in Devon, England, that is also being sold as a seed strain as "*Primula veris* hose-in-hose."

Primula 'Gold-laced' Hose-in-hose

Well this is something quite special and is still difficult to obtain. It is a hose-in-hose form of the Gold-laced polyanthus and is a real primula collector's item as well as being a robust garden plant.

ZONES 4–8

HABIT AND SIZE Polyanthus form. Clump forming. Stem height 8 in. (20 cm).

FLOWERING Early to midspring.

ORIGIN This is one of the prized forms described in old literature and was found in Cannell & Sons catalogue of 1883. Though some forms have occasionally appeared on the show bench in recent years, it is Margaret Webster, holder of a National Plant Collection of *Primula* (British floral variants) in the United Kingdom, who being particularly interested in the anomalous forms, has developed a seed strain of the hose-in-hose form.

LANDSCAPE AND DESIGN USES Don't lose this one in the garden. Good for growing in containers for visual impact.

Primula Jack-in-the-Green Form

Polyanthus Jack-in-the-Green Form, Jack-in-the-pulpit

In these flowers the calyx is transformed into leaves, creating a rosette that offsets the flowers. Both acaulis and polyanthus forms exist with single and double flowers in a very wide range of colours. The green ruff can be quite small so that you hardly notice it to very large. When it becomes very large, the plants can be classified as Galligaskins, named for the wide breeches worn by Tudor and Stuart gentlemen.

ZONES 4–8

HABIT AND SIZE Generally, a polyanthus type though acaulis types do occur. Stem height 8 in. (20 cm).

FLOWERING Late winter to midspring.

ORIGIN Jack-in-the-Greens have been around as natural mutations in the wild for centuries and were popular throughout the seventeenth century and into the eighteenth. There have been many named cultivars through the years, most of which have died out. Barnhaven has had a seed strain on the market since 1948 including these forms and now offers plants in colour strains and a seed mixture. The photo shows a pink form.

LANDSCAPE AND DESIGN USES One of the best primulas for flower arranging.

SIMILAR PLANTS *Primula* Sylvan Series (Jackanapes polyanthus) are a new seed strain available through Owl's Acre speciality seed.

Primula 'Gold-laced Jack-in-the-Green'

This is another unusual form combining a Gold-laced polyanthus and a Jack-in-the-Green form so that the gold-laced mahogany-red flower is nestled in a rosette of green.

ZONES 4–9
HABIT AND SIZE Polyanthus form, clump forming. Stem height 8 in. (20 cm).
FLOWERING Early to midspring.
ORIGIN One of the forms prized by growers in the early 1800s. Several cultivars have been seen over the years, but they are now available as a seed strain from Barnhaven.
LANDSCAPE AND DESIGN USES To be grown in a prominent position in the garden. The flowers also make wonderful posies.
SIMILAR PLANTS *Primula* 'Gold-laced Red Jack-in-the-Green', with a gold-laced brighter red background, is available as seed from Plant World Seeds.

Primula 'Elizabeth Killelay'

A double-flowered Gold-laced polyanthus. Deep-maroon petals are edged in gold with a yellow eye. Vigorous and floriferous, this selection, like most doubles, appreciates some feeding.

ZONES 4–8
HABIT AND SIZE Polyanthus type. Stem height 6 in. (15 cm).
FLOWERING Early to midspring.
ORIGIN This hybrid was discovered in the English garden of Hazel Bolton and named after her young granddaughter.
LANDSCAPE AND DESIGN USES Don't go losing this in your garden undergrowth. It is a stunning plant that needs to be seen. Grow it in containers or in a prominent position.
SIMILAR PLANTS *Primula* 'Tarragem Gilded Garnet' and *P.* 'Tarragem Sparkling Ruby' are double-flowered laced polyanthus bred by Margaret Webster, the first with very gold lacing and the second with a lighter red background to the petals. *Primula* 'Tortoise Shell' has slightly darker flowers than 'Elizabeth Killelay'.

Primula 'Katy McSparron'

SYNONYM *Primula* 'Prinic'

A very distinctive plant as this is a double cowslip with masses of fragrant yellow flowers. It has a long flowering period and is absolutely lovely.

ZONES 3–9
HABIT AND SIZE Polyanthus form. Clump forming. Stem height up to 12 in. (30 cm), so the flower is very visible.
FLOWERING Early to late spring.
ORIGIN Bred by Geoff Nicolle of Wales (in 1989) after years of cross-breeding between *P. veris* and other polyanthus. Named after his granddaughter.
LANDSCAPE AND DESIGN USES Borders and rockeries.

CANDELABRA PRIMULAS

Forget tiny primulas nestling in the hedgerow. Candelabras are gigantic in comparison, growing up to 3 ft. (1 m) tall. They make great marginal plants at the edge of ponds, lakes, and streams and are ideal for boggy areas. They come to us from the high mountain meadows of the Himalayas, but will make themselves perfectly at home in your garden if you have the right conditions.

They also do well under rhododendrons and azaleas, and thrive in damp clearings in woodland. In the garden, they often are planted with grasses, ferns, or hostas. Stunning en masse, candelabras self-sow profusely to create a wonderful mixed palette of colours from orange and yellow to red and pink, even white or dark maroon. If you prefer to grow them in blocks of a single colour, you will have to plant them in different areas of the garden and weed out any plants that appear outside the original colour range.

Primula aurantiaca

A very colourful plant, shorter than other Candelabra primroses, so useful for exposed and windy situations or the
smaller garden. The burnt orange flowers are borne on dark
reddish or even blackish stems and the leaves have red
midribs. Up to 5 or 6 tiers opening in succession. It seems
to appreciate a bit more shade than the other candelabras
and will tolerate slightly drier soil.

ZONES 3–9
HABIT AND SIZE Loses its leaves in winter for self-
protection from the frost. Stem height up to 12 in. (40 cm).
FLOWERING Early to midsummer.
ORIGIN Southwestern China, Myanmar, and Tibet, where it
grows in moist alpine pastures and beside streams.
LANDSCAPE AND DESIGN USES With such striking colours,
this species needs to be planted with companions that will
show it off and not clash. Great with green foliage plants
such as hostas or white-flowering *Astilbe chinensis*.
SIMILAR PLANTS *Primula aurantiaca* × *P. pulverulenta*, an
unnamed hybrid, has scented lilac to red flowers on short
stems of approximately 10 in. (25 cm). It is a compact candelabra, ideal for the smaller garden.

Primula beesiana
Bee's primrose

This species is as easy and vigorous as *P. bulleyana*. The difference is in colour, with lovely pink-purple whorls of yellow-eyed flowers up the white mealy stems. Self-sows abundantly and is quite promiscuous, so if other types of candelabras are in the vicinity, you will soon have a fine array of different coloured offspring.

ZONES 3–9

HABIT AND SIZE Clump forming. Semi-evergreen and dies back to a resting bud. Stem height 28 in. (70 cm).

FLOWERING Late spring to midsummer.

ORIGIN Northwestern Yunnan and southern Sichuan in China.

LANDSCAPE AND DESIGN USES Another great marginal plant for the edges of streams and ponds. Plant with grasses, hostas, irises, mecanopsis, and other Asiatic primulas such as *P. vialii*.

SIMILAR PLANTS *Primula* ×*bulleesiana*, a cross between *P. bulleyana* and *P. beesiana*, has a wide range of colours from pink to mauve, yellow, apricot, and red. It is very hardy and self-sows, providing new colours constantly.

Primula bulleyana
Bulley's primrose

In our experience one of the easiest, most reliable candelabra with glorious crimson buds and pale to deep orange flowers. The leaves have red mid-ribs and the stems are heavily mealed.

ZONES 3–9
HABIT AND SIZE Forms large clumps up to 24 in. (60 cm) across with many stems. Self-seeds freely in good condition. It is semi-evergreen and dies back to a resting bud. Stem height up to 28 in. (70 cm).
FLOWERING Early to midsummer.
ORIGIN The species comes from Yunnan in southwestern China, where it grows in marshes, mountain meadows, and next to streams. It is named after Arthur Kilpin Bulley (1861–1942), an English cotton broker and sponsor of George Forrest (1873–1932), a plant hunter and the discoverer of this plant.

LANDSCAPE AND DESIGN USES As this species flowers slightly later than the majority of candelabra primulas, it can be used to prolong the season of colour in the bog garden or next to a stream or pond. It also works well in a damp, open woodland setting or under tall shrubs where the soil is not too dry.

Primula chungensis

A lovely candelabra notable for its bright crimson buds which open into pale to deep orange flowers in two to five whorls on a silvery mealy stem.

ZONES 3–9

HABIT AND SIZE Clump forming. Stem height up to 24 in. (60 cm).

FLOWERING Early summer.

ORIGIN From the mountainous regions of China, India, and Tibet. Found along streamsides and marshlands.

LANDSCAPE AND DESIGN USES Excellent with other woodland plants such as camellia or rhododendron, or as a marginal plant.

SIMILAR PLANTS *Primula* ×*chunglenta*, a cross between *P. chungensis* and *P. pulverulenta*, is a vigorous plant with pinky red flowers and a darker eye.

Primula cockburniana

A very dainty candelabra with just one to three whorls of flaming orange flowers. We always look forward to its flowering. Not at all brash like some of the other candelabras, this delicate plant is simply charming with lots of silvery flowering stems to each individual. It is not the most enduring of plants and often needs to be replaced every couple of years, but it's very easy to gather its seed and re-sow to replenish stocks.

ZONES 3–9

HABIT AND SIZE Makes small clumps. Loses its leaves in winter, so don't dig it up by mistake. Stem height 15 in. (40 cm).

FLOWERING Early to midsummer.

ORIGIN Southwestern Sichuan in China, in marshy alpine meadows. Discovered in 1886, introduced into cultivation in 1905, and grown ever since.

LANDSCAPE AND DESIGN USES With such a vibrant orange colour, this primrose must be carefully sited in the garden. Try putting a group in front of a bed of yellow or creamy white rhododendrons, or at the front of a damp border with ornamental grasses or ferns.

SIMILAR PLANTS *Primula cockburniana* 'Kevock Sunshine' is an unusual yellow form with two or three whorls of flowers up the stem.

Primula Harlow Car hybrids

Primula Harlow Car hybrids produce tall whorls of yellow, peach, pink, or soft purple flowers. They can make a startling display when planted in large swathes of mixed colours and will self-seed profusely.

ZONES 3–9

HABIT AND SIZE Very large leaves, which die down in winter to protect the plants from frost. Large clump forming. Stem height 24 in. (60 cm).

FLOWERING Early to midsummer.

ORIGIN These hybrids appeared when *Primula bulleyana*, *P. beesiana*, and *P. pulverulenta* were planted in close proximity in the RHS Harlow Carr gardens. They cross-bred and popped up all over the garden, often in full sun. The seed has been on sale since the 1960s. (The hybrids were first recorded as 'Harlow Car' with a single *r* and the name has stuck ever since.)

LANDSCAPE AND DESIGN USES At Harlow Carr, they grow along a stream where you will also find *Lysichiton americanus*, *Athyrium niponicum* 'Pictum', *Primula florindae*, and *Matteuccia struthiopteris*. They will do well as the centrepiece of a bog garden.

SIMILAR PLANTS *Primula japonica* Oriental Sunrise Group is a Barnhaven strain with a superb array of flower colours ranging from the palest peach, coral, and pink through to burnt orange. When most of the other candelabras are over, Oriental Sunrise is just beginning and makes a lovely display in the middle of summer. *Primula* Inshriach Hybrids, bred by Jack Drake in Scotland, also come in similar shades of orange and pink.

Primula 'Inverewe'

The colour makes this candelabra stand out. It has six or seven whorls of clear scarlet to brilliant orange flowers with an orange eye which contrast well with the white powdery stem.

ZONES 3–9
HABIT AND SIZE Clump forming, but doesn't set seed so must be propagated by division. Stem height 24 in. (60 cm).
FLOWERING Late spring to early summer.
ORIGIN A hybrid between *P. pulverulenta* and *P. cockburniana* first found at Inverewe Garden in Scotland.
LANDSCAPE AND DESIGN USES The bright colours of this candelabra have to be carefully placed but combine well with other yellow candelabras or shade-loving plants such as dark-leaved *Actaea simplex* 'James Compton'.

Primula japonica 'Apple Blossom'

Japanese primrose 'Apple Blossom'

A delightful plant with whorls of soft pink apple blossom flowers with a red eye. There are always nuances of shades within the pink colour palette, which make a mass of these flowers very pleasing to the eye.

ZONES 3–9

HABIT AND SIZE Clump forming. These are perennial plants which lose their leaves in the winter so don't worry when they disappear late in autumn. Stem height 24 in. (60 cm).

FLOWERING Late spring to early summer.

ORIGIN As the name might suggest, *P. japonica* was introduced to the West from Japan in the 1870s. Usually with purple-red flowers in the wild, 'Apple Blossom' is one of the nicest colour strains that has been bred since that time.

LANDSCAPE AND DESIGN USES Plant it in drifts or groups, never singly, with hostas, iris, and ferns in damp open woodland, next to streams or ponds. Enjoying the same soil requirements, it does also does well under rhododendrons and azaleas, which give the primula some dappled shade.

SIMILAR PLANTS *Primula japonica* 'Glowing Embers' has magenta pink flowers.

Primula japonica 'Miller's Crimson'

Japanese primrose 'Miller's Crimson'

This is one of the earliest flowering candelabras, with true crimson or dark red flowers that grow in one to six whorls up the stem. Although this primrose grows in full sun in very wet conditions, the sun can bleach the flowers, so semi-shade is preferable. It has been described as one of the easiest primulas to grow and is widely available. It is distinguishable from many other similar strains by its non-mealy stems.

ZONES 3–9

HABIT AND SIZE Forms big clumps in moist soil, with very large leaves, so don't plant too close together. The leaves die down to a resting bud in winter. Stem height to 24 in. (60 cm).

FLOWERING Late spring to early summer.

ORIGIN A selection of the widespread Japanese species, which grows in boggy places next to mountain streams.

LANDSCAPE AND DESIGN USES Magnificent in mass plantings in damp woodland areas, next to a stream or pond. It is early flowering so can be used with ferns and spring bulbs or ornamental grasses. Self-sowing in good conditions, it can quickly fill up an area to great effect.

SIMILAR PLANTS *Primula japonica* 'Carminea' is a vigorous cultivar with deep carmine red flowers. *Primula japonica* 'Valley Red' has nearly scarlet flowers with an orange eye.

Primula japonica 'Postford White'

White Japanese primrose, white candelabra

One of our favourite candelabras, bearing one to six whorls of fresh white flowers with an orange eye. A perennial primula that self-sows abundantly. Not difficult and widely available.

ZONES 3–9

HABIT AND SIZE Forms large clumps and then dies down completely to a resting bud in winter. Stem height 24 in. (60 cm).

FLOWERING Late spring to early summer.

ORIGIN A selection of *Primula japonica* originally widely distributed throughout Japan. Introduced in 1870 and has been grown in the West ever since.

LANDSCAPE AND DESIGN USES One of the earliest candelabras to flower, it can be used to great effect with spring bulbs, hostas, and ferns in damp shady beds or in marginal plantings next to ponds and streams. We like it in combination with the variegated grass *Phalaris arundinacea* var. *picta* 'Feesey', which tolerates damp conditions (be aware it can be invasive in certain areas though).

SIMILAR PLANTS *Primula japonica* 'Alba' has pure white flowers or white with a yellow or pink eye.

Primula prolifera

Marsh primula, glory of the bog
SYNONYMS *Primula helodoxa, P. smithiana*

An outstanding example of a candelabra primula, with the brightest of bright yellow flowers and one of the very tallest. It also is one of the latest candelabras to flower and makes a great companion for the equally tardy orange shades. Unusual in that it has evergreen leaves so is less likely to be dug up by mistake in winter. This is a true bog primula that will stand very wet conditions.

ZONES 3–9

HABIT AND SIZE Forms large clumps. Stem height 38–48 in. (100–120 cm). Very variable in the wild. Some plants with stems only half as tall were once known as a separate species, *P. smithiana*.

FLOWERING Early to midsummer.

ORIGIN Northeastern Myanmar and China, in streamsides and damp alpine meadows.

LANDSCAPE AND DESIGN USES *Primula prolifera* gives great structural height to the garden. Use it with ferns and grasses in your boggy patches, next to a pond or stream, or in moist areas under tall shrubs. It is breathtaking with Japanese irises and can also be grown in a container—if you use a very large deep container such as an old zinc tub.

Primula pulverulenta
Mealy primrose

An absolutely stunning plant when planted en masse, this is one of the most widely grown candelabras. It is easy to grow and self-seeds readily. It bears several whorls of dark cerise to wine-red flowers. The dark flowers contrast with the silver-powdered stems and buds.

ZONES 3–9

HABIT AND SIZE Forms large clumps. Dies back to a resting bud in the winter. Stem height 2–3 ft. (60–90 cm).

FLOWERING Late spring to early summer.

CULTIVATION Prefers semi-shade but tolerates full sun if grown in very damp conditions. Needs moist to wet humus-rich soil but does not appreciate sitting in water in the winter.

ORIGIN From western Sichuan in China, where it grows in damp or wet meadows. *Pulverulenta* is derived from the Latin *pulvis* meaning "dust" in reference to the powdery covering.

LANDSCAPE AND DESIGN USES A great marginal plant at the edge of ponds, lakes, and streams but also in woodland and borders. Often used in combination with other candelabras and grasses, ferns, or hostas.

SIMILAR PLANTS *Primula pulverulenta* Bartley hybrids were introduced by G. H. Dalrymple of Bartley Nurseries in the 1920s. They are lovely hybrids with flowers in shell pink shades and with very mealy stems and buds.

Primula wilsonii

Primula wilsonii is a useful candelabra with dark green shiny leaves and whorls of small cup-shaped purple flowers. The foliage is said to smell of aniseed (anise), but not very strongly so.

ZONES 3–9

HABIT AND SIZE Evergreen, so less likely to disappear by overly enthusiastic weeding in winter. Forms large clumps. Stem height up to 35 in. (90 cm).

FLOWERING Early to midsummer.

ORIGIN First discovered in 1822, it is found in damp meadows in southwestern China.

LANDSCAPE AND DESIGN USES Planting candelabras provides that very useful colour in midsummer. Very much at home on the borders of streams and ponds, they can also be planted in shady damp parts of a border, preferably north- or east-facing. We have also used them in deep zinc containers with grasses and ferns.

SIMILAR PLANTS *Primula wilsonii* var. *anisodora* is an interesting variation with almost black buds and dark red flowers. It too has evergreen leaves. The stout stems are up to 24 in. (60 cm) tall. *Primula poissonii* is another candelabra with evergreen leaves, a similar port, and thin stems, but the flowers are very bright rich pink.

BELLED PRIMULAS

Interesting because they bloom from late spring to midsummer, with some continuing into autumn, belled primulas are very attractive, with gently drooping bell-like flowers, many of them highly scented. They die down completely in the winter, but in spring make clumps of rounded leaves. Then the flower stems grow, each bearing two or three large whorls of flowers in a range of white, cream, orange, red, maroon, or purple with the insides often covered in cream powder. Most species are from the western Himalayas, but are also found growing in central Nepal, Myanmar, and Gansu province in China. Because the flowers are carried on tall stems, single plants can look a bit leggy. It is always best to plant these in a group. They make wonderful marginal plants next to a pond or in the bog garden, accompanied by candelabra primulas or ornamental grasses. They also grow well in woodland conditions or in small groups in a border.

Primula alpicola
Moonlight primrose

Although this species is called a belled primula, its flowers resemble a Chinese coolie's hat more than a bell. Large blooms of soft yellow, violet, white, mauve, and occasionally raspberry are dusted with creamy meal within. They have a very heady scent and when in bloom in our growing tunnels in summer, the fragrance is almost overpowering.

ZONES 3–9
HABIT AND SIZE The leaves die down completely in winter and re-emerge in spring to make clumps. Stem height to 18 in. (45 cm).
FLOWERING Early to midsummer.
ORIGIN Southwestern China, Bhutan, northeastern India, from wet mountain meadows and streamsides.
LANDSCAPE AND DESIGN USES Although it likes damp conditions, it does not like to be waterlogged, so if planting near water, place it where it won't get flooded.
SIMILAR PLANTS Three varieties of this species are known: var. *alba*, gentle white flower ◀; var. *luna*, pale yellow flower; and var. *violacea*, purple, pink, or violet flower with white meal inside ▼.

Primula florindae
Giant cowslip, Tibetan cowslip

The largest primula in the world, making huge clumps in wet conditions. With spicy fragrant mops of sulphur yellow bells, this superb plant is a must for the middle of summer. It freely self-seeds, and the seedlings are quite easy to recognize as the leaves are heart shaped at the base, and the roots, if you happen to look, are red. If you can choose only one primula to grow by your garden pond, this would have to be it.

ZONES 3–9

HABIT AND SIZE Deciduous. Tolerates being waterlogged. Stem height to 4 ft. (1.2 m).

FLOWERING Midsummer.

ORIGIN Southeastern Tibet, in forest bogs and streambeds.

LANDSCAPE AND DESIGN USES *Primula florindae* reaches its full potential in wet conditions and makes an impact on the landscape if planted in drifts. It and its hybrids are marginal plants and tolerate occasional flooding if planted by a stream or pond. In the damp border, they can be grown with other primulas such as *P. alpicola*, *P. sikkimensis*, or *P. vialii*.

SIMILAR PLANTS Hybrids of this species can be found in lovely shades of russet, burnt orange, raspberry red, and even pink.

Primula secundiflora

A beautiful plant. Very easy to recognize by the dark purple and white stripy calyx and lovely reddish purple bell-shaped flowers. The stem is mealed with silver, creating a striking contrast.

ZONES 3–9
HABIT AND SIZE Forms large rosettes of slim, light green evergreen leaves and is very long lived in good conditions. Self-sows readily. Stem height up to 3 ft. (90 cm).
FLOWERING Early to midsummer.
ORIGIN From the high mountains of northwestern Yunnan and south-western Sichuan in China, where it is found in ditches and beside streams.
LANDSCAPE AND DESIGN USES A great marginal plant for streams and ponds, and also for damp boggy patches where it never dries out.

Primula sikkimensis

Sikkim cowslip

A vigorous and reliable plant with soft flaring bells of yellow or creamy white flowers. This is a true bog garden plant and fragrant, too.

ZONES 3–9
HABIT AND SIZE Makes large clumps and often self-sows. Stem height up to 35 in. (90 cm).
FLOWERING Early to midsummer.
ORIGIN In the wild, it is one of the most widespread primulas, found in Nepal, southwestern China, India, and Tibet, which accounts for there being quite wide variation in the species. It grows in wet alpine-meadows and streamsides, usually in glacial valleys. First introduced into cultivation by English botanist William J. Hooker in 1849.
LANDSCAPE AND DESIGN USES As a marginal plant on the edges of streams or ponds, or also in shady damp beds. In the wild, it often grows with *P. secundiflora*.
SIMILAR PLANTS There are many *P. sikkimensis* hybrids, probably the results of crosses with *P. waltonii* or *P. alpicola* var. *violacea*, which can be nearly pink in colour with white meal.

Primula waltonii
Ruby primula

Primula waltonii has sharply toothed leaves and bears umbels of pendant, dark lilac to reddish purple flowers with mealy edges. The flowers are deliciously fragrant.

ZONES 3–9
HABIT AND SIZE Deciduous. Stem height to 20 in. (50 cm).
FLOWERING Early to midsummer.
ORIGIN It was discovered by Captain H. J. Walton in Tibet where it grows on wet alpine meadows.
LANDSCAPE AND DESIGN USES Plant with *P. alpicola* or *P. secundiflora* as marginal plants at the edge of a stream or in damp woodland.
SIMILAR PLANTS *Primula ioessa* also has bell-shaped flowers that range from white, pale pink, and lilac blue through to violet, with meal inside the bell. It is also fragrant but not as tall as *P. waltonii*. It seems to be relatively short-lived in the garden (about three years), but is easily replenished from seed.

PRIMULA SIEBOLDII

Known as Siebold's primrose, cherry blossom primrose, or Japanese woodland primrose, *P. sieboldii* is the ultimate plant for any shady corner or woodland garden where it romps about without becoming invasive. In Japan, where it is known as sakurasō, it is often grown in a pot. It makes great cut flowers.

Primula sieboldii should feature in many more gardens as it has so much going for it including slightly hairy, crinkly leaves and slender stems bearing several flowers in whorls in shades of pink, white, blue, and everything in between. Despite its dainty appearance, it is a glorious garden plant that can put up with more extremes in temperature than other primula because of the long dormant period. It resists drought, subzero temperatures, and a fair amount of neglect.

The species comes in a multitude of beautiful forms, including more than 400 named cultivars and seed strains, which makes it seriously collectable. It was very difficult to choose which specific named cultivars to recommend as there are so many out there and names are not always reliable. In our humble opinion as serious sieboldii fans, we would grow them all if we could. The small selection of plants described here gives you an idea of the variety that is available, but just give them a try and enjoy the huge diversity that they offer.

Primula sieboldii 'Akatonbo'

This cultivar has deep pink small flowers with white spots around the centre. The petals are narrow and have a snowflake form.

ZONES 4–8
HABIT AND SIZE Rosette forming, deciduous. Creeping rootstock. Stem height 8–10 in. (20–25 cm).
FLOWERING Late spring to early summer.
ORIGIN This Japanese cultivar dates back to the end of the nineteenth century. Its name means "red dragonfly."
LANDSCAPE AND DESIGN USES Woodland gardens, shady borders, and containers.
SIMILAR PLANTS *Primula sieboldii* Romance Group is a Barnhaven strain that is also a deep pink with frilly petals and the characteristic stronger and slightly shorter stems than the Japanese varieties. *Primula sieboldii* 'Bureikō', from Japan, has deep pink flowers with a white spot at the centre and very lacy, snowflake petals.

Primula sieboldii
Dancing Ladies Group

Many cultivars of *P. sieboldii* have a different colour on the reverse of the petals. This is one of them, having very frilly petals with white on the outside and pink on the reverse.

ZONES 4–8 (reportedly even zone 3)
HABIT AND SIZE Rosette forming, deciduous. Creeping rootstock. Stem height 12 in. (30 cm).
FLOWERING Late spring to early summer.
ORIGIN A Barnhaven seed strain.
LANDSCAPE AND DESIGN USES Woodland gardens, shady borders, and containers.
SIMILAR PLANTS *Primula sieboldii* 'Chubby One', an American selection by Seneca Hills Perennials, also has white-faced flowers flushed pink on the reverse (though admittedly the name doesn't do the flower justice). *Primula sieboldii* 'Isotaka', a Japanese cultivar, has lovely, lacy, pink-edged white flowers backed in pink.

Primula sieboldii 'Kashima'

This cultivar has large flowers with frilly snowflake petals that are suffused with mauve concentrated toward the centre of the flower. The reverse side is pink suffused. A stunning variety that is a fairly vigorous despite its fragile appearance.

ZONES 4–8

HABIT AND SIZE Rosette forming, deciduous. Creeping rootstock. Stem height 8–10 in. (20–25 cm).

FLOWERING Late spring to early summer.

ORIGIN A Japanese cultivar. The name means "Deer Island."

LANDSCAPE AND DESIGN USES Woodland gardens, shady borders, and containers.

SIMILAR PLANTS *Primula sieboldii* Trade Winds Group is a Barnhaven seed strain that has very frilly petals suffused with mauve-blue. The reverse side of the petals is often blue.

Primula sieboldii
Manakoora Group

This strain is characterised by smooth, round flowers in various shades of lavender and light blue. There are many named clones on the market with different forms of blue that have originated from this strain. We find that the blue strains are not as vigorous as some of the other colours, though they are just as hardy. They often seem to have slightly longer stems than our other strains.

ZONES 4–8
HABIT AND SIZE Rosette forming, deciduous. Creeping rootstock. Stem height 8–10 in. (20–25 cm).
FLOWERING Late spring to early summer.
ORIGIN A Barnhaven seed strain.
LANDSCAPE AND DESIGN USES Woodland gardens, shady borders, and containers.
SIMILAR PLANTS *Primula sieboldii* Gloaming Group is another strain introduced by Barnhaven in the 1970s with dark blue, lavender shades. *Primula sieboldii* 'Blue Lagoon', a named clone that has blue tinted pink flowers with a suffused white middle, was introduced by Blooms of Bressingham.

Primula sieboldii 'Nankinkozakura'

We had to include this one just because it is one of the oldest cultivars around. It dates back to the early eighteenth century. How's that for a piece of history? If it has survived this long, it must be vigorous. It has smaller flowers than many of the other cultivars. The flowers are dark pink with a white edge and we find they come into bloom slightly earlier than many of our own hybrids.

ZONES 4–8

HABIT AND SIZE Rosette forming, deciduous. Creeping rootstock. Stem height 8–10 in. (20–25 cm).

FLOWERING Late spring to early summer.

ORIGIN A Japanese cultivar. It is mentioned in a book by Ihei Ito, a nurseryman in the Tokyo area, in 1733. Its name means "primula of Nankin" (the Chinese town—literally, the capital of the South).

LANDSCAPE AND DESIGN USES Woodland gardens, shady borders, and containers.

SIMILAR PLANTS *Primula sieboldii* 'Sumizomegenji' is an old cultivar with small flowers and a distinctive white edge, but the flowers are of a purple/magenta colour.

Primula sieboldii
Nirvana Group

Flowers are a light marshmallow pink with smooth rounded petals. Some have a white centre.

ZONES 4–8

HABIT AND SIZE Rosette forming, deciduous. Creeping rootstock. Stem height 8 in. (20 cm).

FLOWERING Late spring to early summer.

ORIGIN A Barnhaven seed strain.

LANDSCAPE AND DESIGN USES Woodland gardens, shady borders, and containers. The light pink colours are lovely in combination with the white smooth varieties of *P. sieboldii* Pale Moon Group.

SIMILAR PLANTS Many named cultivars of *P. sieboldii* are a similar light pink colour such as 'Blush Pink', 'Sorcha's Pink', or 'Spring Blush'. *Primula sieboldii* 'Martin Nest Pink' has large flowers and was raised by Mary Robinson of Martin Nest Nurseries in the United Kingdom.

Primula sieboldii Pago-Pago Group

A dark pink-magenta strain with smooth, rounded petals often with a white centre. There are also selected forms from this strain being sold as named cultivars.

ZONES 4–8
HABIT AND SIZE Rosette forming, deciduous. Creeping rootstock. Stem height 8 in. (20 cm).
FLOWERING Late spring to early summer.
ORIGIN A Barnhaven seed strain.
LANDSCAPE AND DESIGN USES Woodland gardens, shady borders, and containers.
SIMILAR PLANTS *Primula sieboldii* 'Aaimayama', a Japanese cultivar, has pink flowers with a white centre and very pronounced notched petals. *Primula sieboldii* 'Geisha Girl', a light pink European hybrid with a white centre and white tracings on the veins, is widely available in the United Kingdom and has been around for some years as it was first listed by Blooms of Bressingham in 1969.

Primula sieboldii 'Seneca Star'

This cultivar has large flowers with frilly petals that are fringed with pink, creating a white star-like pattern in the centre. It is said by everyone who grows it to be very vigorous.

ZONES 4–8
HABIT AND SIZE Rosette forming, deciduous. Creeping rootstock. Stem height 8–10 in. (20–25 cm).
FLOWERING Late spring to early summer.
ORIGIN An American selection made by Ellen Hornig of Seneca Hills Perennials (no longer trading) and introduced in 2008.
LANDSCAPE AND DESIGN USES Woodland gardens, shady borders, and containers.
SIMILAR PLANTS *Primula sieboldii* 'Carefree' has pink flowers with a white centre and white traced veins but has round (smooth) petals.

Primula sieboldii Snowbird Group

The flowers in this strain have pure white frilly snowflake petals, though there are many other frilly white forms on the market. In our experience, this is one of the most vigorous strains with strong stems and a shorter habit.

ZONES 4–8

HABIT AND SIZE Rosette forming, deciduous. Creeping rootstock. Stem height 8–10 in. (20–25 cm).

FLOWERING Late spring to early summer.

ORIGIN A Barnhaven strain formerly known as 'Winter Dreams' which has been now separated into frilly and smooth forms.

LANDSCAPE AND DESIGN USES Woodland gardens and shady borders. These are lovely in combination with blue bells or the white-and-blue columbine *Aquilegia flabellata*.

SIMILAR PLANTS You will find many frilly white hybrids with much variation in petal shape. Some of these are simply sold as *P. sieboldii* 'White' or 'Snowflake'. *Primula sieboldii* 'Late Snow' is a very feathered, pure white selection with large blooms. *Primula sieboldii* 'Syosin' is a Japanese hybrid of pure white lacy flowers which are slightly larger than usual.

Primula sieboldii 'Snowdrop'

This selection produces umbels of five pure white flowers with smooth edges and large petals. It has been micro-propagated, and although it is a slightly untidy plant, we are recommending it as it is widely available though there are many other smooth white varieties that are just as good if not better.

ZONES 4–8

HABIT AND SIZE Rosette forming, deciduous. Creeping rootstock. Stem height 12 in. (30 cm).

FLOWERING Late spring to early summer.

ORIGIN Unknown

LANDSCAPE AND DESIGN USES Woodland gardens, shady borders, and containers. A dream in combination with other dark foliage plants or hostas.

SIMILAR PLANTS *Primula sieboldii* 'Ginhukurin' is a vigorous Japanese cultivar with pure white flowers and the faintest rose flush in the centre. The name means silver-coloured ring. *Primula sieboldii* 'Snowflake' is another pure white smooth form though just to confuse things you also find 'Snowflake' sold as a frilly form. *Primula sieboldii* Pale Moon Group is a Barnhaven seed strain with round smooth white flowers.

Primula sieboldii Tah-ni Group

A frilly light pink strain. These dainty flowers look magical in the garden.

ZONES 4–8
HABIT AND SIZE Rosette forming, deciduous. Creeping rootstock. Stem height 8 in. (20 cm).
FLOWERING Late spring to early summer.
ORIGIN A Barnhaven seed strain.
LANDSCAPE AND DESIGN USES Woodland gardens, shady borders, and containers.
SIMILAR PLANTS *Primula sieboldii* 'Edomurasaki' is a Japanese cultivar with pale pink feathered flowers with a white centre. It has very slender notched petals.

OTHER SPECIES

It is so hard to choose from the hundreds of *Primula* species that exist, and we are sure there are plenty of primula lovers who will hold their hands up in horror because we have missed their favorite one. But not all of those species are very easy to grow, so we have chosen some of the easiest, most outstanding species that are readily available and that perform well in the garden. You will be astonished that some of them belong in the genus *Primula*. Who would guess that *P. vialii*, the red hot poker primrose, is related to the common hedgerow primrose, until you look at the leaves, and that's a giveaway. *Primula denticulata*, the drumstick primrose, is another, with its startling round balls of flowers that resemble allium flowers. It is quite well known, but not always recognized as being a primrose cousin. Each of these species needs different conditions in the garden, which we have detailed for each entry.

Primula capitata subsp. *mooreana*

Such a striking plant with grey-blue foliage, stalk and leaves heavily dusted with farina, and the flower head resembling a slighted flattened globe, where just the outer ring of flowers matures. It has a gentle fragrance.

ZONES 3–9

HABIT AND SIZE Will live probably for a maximum of three seasons, so better planted in groups that will then set seed for you to replenish the stock. Leaves reduce to a small rosette in winter. Stem height up to 18 in. (45 cm).

FLOWERING Late spring and, depending on its situation and conditions, often giving a second show in late summer or even in autumn.

CULTIVATION Not a difficult plant to grow in the garden. It needs good light, but should not be allowed to dry out. The soil should be well drained, but containing plenty of humus to maintain moisture. If necessary, the plant is easy to divide after flowering.

ORIGIN Widespread in high alpine situations in Nepal, China, Tibet, and Bhutan.

LANDSCAPE AND DESIGN USES As a marginal plant with hostas, grasses, irises, and mecanopsis. In the herbaceous border, slightly shaded. Also lovely in containers with silver-foliaged plants.

SIMILAR PLANTS *Primula glomerata* is very similar and the foliage is quite difficult to tell apart, but the flower forms a complete globe and often leans to one side. *Primula capitata* 'Noverna Deep Blue' is readily available in seed form.

Primula chionantha

This species emerges from a resting bud in late spring and the elongated leaves are covered in an attractive white or yellow meal. The velvety purple-blue, lilac, or white flowers appear on stout stems in umbels. When it is grown in the right position in the garden, it can be stunning.

ZONES 3–8

HABIT AND SIZE Deciduous. Forms large clumps with several crowns that can be divided in the autumn. Stem height up to 1 ft. (30 cm).

FLOWERING Late spring to early summer.

CULTIVATION A vigorous plant in the garden that flowers readily. It prefers a semi-shaded cool and sheltered position. It will thrive in humus-rich, fertile, damp soil but not waterlogged in the winter.

ORIGIN From mountainous regions of western China, Yunnan, Sichuan, and Tibet, often seen growing among dwarf rhododendrons.

LANDSCAPE AND DESIGN USES Can be grown in a bog garden or in a damp border.

SIMILAR PLANTS *Primula macrophylla* is similar and is often seen in cultivation in its purple form. It is more short-lived in the garden, but sets seeds readily when grown in groups.

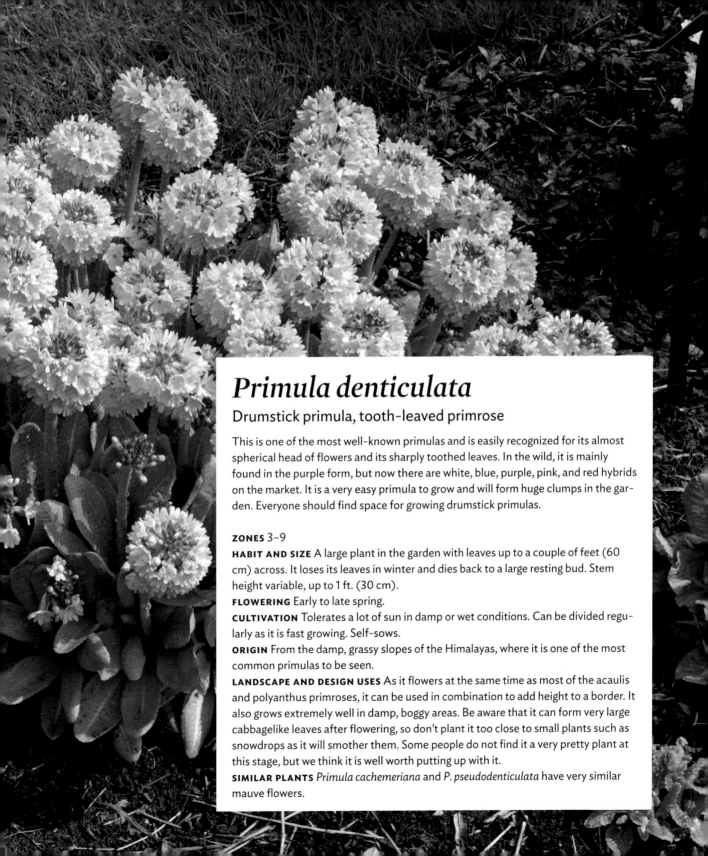

Primula denticulata

Drumstick primula, tooth-leaved primrose

This is one of the most well-known primulas and is easily recognized for its almost spherical head of flowers and its sharply toothed leaves. In the wild, it is mainly found in the purple form, but now there are white, blue, purple, pink, and red hybrids on the market. It is a very easy primula to grow and will form huge clumps in the garden. Everyone should find space for growing drumstick primulas.

ZONES 3–9

HABIT AND SIZE A large plant in the garden with leaves up to a couple of feet (60 cm) across. It loses its leaves in winter and dies back to a large resting bud. Stem height variable, up to 1 ft. (30 cm).

FLOWERING Early to late spring.

CULTIVATION Tolerates a lot of sun in damp or wet conditions. Can be divided regularly as it is fast growing. Self-sows.

ORIGIN From the damp, grassy slopes of the Himalayas, where it is one of the most common primulas to be seen.

LANDSCAPE AND DESIGN USES As it flowers at the same time as most of the acaulis and polyanthus primroses, it can be used in combination to add height to a border. It also grows extremely well in damp, boggy areas. Be aware that it can form very large cabbagelike leaves after flowering, so don't plant it too close to small plants such as snowdrops as it will smother them. Some people do not find it a very pretty plant at this stage, but we think it is well worth putting up with it.

SIMILAR PLANTS *Primula cachemeriana* and *P. pseudodenticulata* have very similar mauve flowers.

Primula grandis

SYNONYM *Sredinskya grandis*

Although this plant is not to everyone's taste, we think it is a lot of fun. We have found it very easy to grow and the flowers are extremely unusual. In fact, it has only recently been classified as a *Primula* as the tube-shaped flowers don't resemble any other plant in this genus. The small yellow flowers are borne on large nodding clusters of up to 30 individuals. It forms a statuesque plant in the right conditions. Although it is not often seen in cultivation, we feel more people should be finding it a home.

ZONES 3–9
HABIT AND SIZE Large leaves up to 12 in. (30 cm) across, deciduous. Stem height up to 15 in. (40 cm), stems mealy.
FLOWERING Late spring to early summer.
CULTIVATION Grows in sun to part shade. It likes the same conditions as the candelabra primulas, with plenty of water in the growing period. It has a very thin rootstock that seems to divide easily.
ORIGIN Wet alpine meadows and banks of mountain streams in the western end of the Caucasian chain.
LANDSCAPE AND DESIGN USES Can be used as a marginal plant in a bog garden, or in a damp border.

Primula kisoana

With its hairy leaves and delicate bright flowers, this is a very distinctive plant. The pink form seems to be commonly grown in the United States, whereas the white form seems more popular in Europe, but they are both equally vigorous in our experience.

ZONES 5–8

HABIT AND SIZE Deciduous leaves and creeping roots. Self-seeds to form colonies. Stem height up to 8 in. (20 cm).

FLOWERING Mid to late spring.

CULTIVATION Prefers part shade, in a humus-rich, damp but well-drained soil. May suffer in very warm climates where it is best grown in complete shade. Doesn't need dividing that much as it will spread out on its rhizomes.

ORIGIN Native to Japan. Original collection at Mount Kiso, hence its name. It is now listed as an endangered species in Japan.

LANDSCAPE AND DESIGN USES This delightful woodland plant forms a lovely ground cover when left to run, but it is decidous, so there will be nothing to see in the winter months.

SIMILAR PLANTS *Primula jesoana* has slightly longer stems and doesn't share its creeping rootstock. *Primula kisoana* var. *shikokiana* 'Iyobeni' is a wonderful clear red Japanese cultivar.

Primula munroi

This little plant always surprises us with its powerful scent. It makes mats of small spoon-shaped leaves with relatively tall stems. The flowers are variable and, although they are usually white, you will find some tinged with pink or even purple.

ZONES 4–8
HABIT AND SIZE A compact perennial which loses its leaves in winter. Stem height up to 12 in. (30 cm).
FLOWERING Late spring to early summer.
CULTIVATION Prefers dappled shade unless in a damp position where it tolerates more sun. Likes a moist but free-draining soil. It can be divided into individual rosettes as the leaves re-appear in midspring.
ORIGIN Widespread in the Himalayas, usually found in moist alpine meadows near streams.
LANDSCAPE AND DESIGN USES As this is a delicate-looking plant (though actually very robust), place it where it won't be overwhelmed by larger types, for instance, at the front of a boggy patch, with larger bog plants behind it, such as *P. bulleyana*, *P. florindae*, and irises.
SIMILAR PLANTS *Primula munroi* subsp. *yargongensis* has purple or deep pink flowers.

Primula parryi
Parry's primrose

This robust plant can be among the largest of primulas when grown in the right conditions. It has a distinctive, unpleasant smell and long dark thick green leaves. It flowers profusely, producing bright magenta flowers with a yellow eye.

ZONES 3–9

HABIT AND SIZE Very long leaves up to 12 in. (30 cm). Stem height up to 15 in. (40 cm).

FLOWERING Late spring to early summer.

CULTIVATION Grows in part shade but tolerates full sun when grown in wet places. Best kept very wet in summer and on the dry side in winter (as it is usually covered in snow).

ORIGIN This is one of the few American native species and can be found in many areas of the Rocky Mountains and from Montana to Arizona and New Mexico. Generally found on wet places on mountains usually above the tree line. Named for *Charles Christopher Parry*, director of Kew Gardens in England, who discovered it in 1861.

LANDSCAPE AND DESIGN USES Along streamsides and next to ponds. Tolerates being waterlogged.

Primula rosea 'Grandiflora'
Rosy primrose, marsh primrose

A popular primula which provides a vivid splash of very early colour in the garden. The flowers form brilliant shocking pink cushions which blossom the minute the buds come through the ground, even before the flower stalk has grown. Very eye-catching from afar.

ZONES 3–9
HABIT AND SIZE After flowering produces many leaves, which subsequently disappear in winter. Freely self-sows in good conditions. Stem height up to 4 in. (10 cm), but taller when carrying seeds.
FLOWERING Early to midspring.
CULTIVATION Grows in sun to light shade. Delights in a wet, boggy soil, such as on a river bank, but can also be grown in ordinary garden conditions if not too dry. Can be divided every year or so after flowering. Seed needs to be sown very fresh to succeed.
ORIGIN Northwestern Himalayas in alpine pastures and meadow.
LANDSCAPE AND DESIGN USES This primula thrives even in the wettest places and can be used for very early colour in a dank, moist corner.
SIMILAR PLANTS *Primula rosea* 'Delight' is, in theory, an improved selection of 'Grandiflora'. *Primula rosea* 'Micia Visser-de Geer' has darker pink, almost carmine flowers.

Primula scotica
Scottish primrose

A true native of Scotland, this dainty plant has blue-grey leaves from which emerge rich, dark purple flowers that are sweetly scented. The leaves and stem are covered with an attractive whitish meal.

ZONES 4–8

HABIT AND SIZE Neat and small, forming compact rosettes of leaves. The flowers emerge before the stalks. Stem height to 3 in. (7 cm).

FLOWERING Early summer, but oftens flowers in late spring in the wild.

CULTIVATION The species is best grown in groups for cross pollination and is ideal in a trough or shallow pot. It prefers some shade in the summer and requires a gritty soil or compost which retains moisture. Can be divided after flowering, but is not quick growing.

ORIGIN Endemic to the north coast of Scotland and found only in Orkney, Caithness, and Sutherland, where it grows in stony turf and on cliff tops.

LANDSCAPE AND DESIGN USES Plant in an old sink or trough with marginata hybrids or dwarf muscari. A tiny delight, it needs to be where you can see and appreciate it.

SIMILAR PLANTS *Primula farinosa*, bird's-eye primrose, is another European species with a lilac or pink flower. *Primula halleri* is larger than *P. scotica* with a lilac to violet flower.

Primula vialii

Vial's, Chinese, pagoda, poker, or wayside primrose

One of the most recognizable primulas and perhaps the most surprising as it couldn't be more different from the humble primrose of the hedgerows. Somewhat resembling a red hot poker, the spike emerges bright red and then slowly turns to blue-violet from the base upward so that eventually there are lavender flowers with a crimson tip.

ZONES 3–9

HABIT AND SIZE Loses its leaves in winter, but they emerge again in late spring. Said to be difficult to keep unless the conditions are right, but well worth the effort. Very easy to renew from seed, either commercial or by just keeping the seed heads at the end of summer. Stem height to 24 in. (60 cm).

FLOWERING Early summer.

CULTIVATION Can be grown in direct sun if the soil is moist enough but otherwise needs some shade. Requires a fertile, humus-rich, moist soil. It can be divided although more often it is propagated by new seed.

ORIGIN From the damp meadows of southwestern China.

LANDSCAPE AND DESIGN USES Often grown in drifts under rhododendron bushes, or in clearings in damp woodland or copses. A large number of plants grown together have a huge impact.

SIMILAR PLANTS *Primula flaccida* has spikes of lavender flowers on stems up to 20 in. (50 cm) tall. A striking plant but not as easy to grow.

ALPINE PRIMULAS

If you want some early colour at the end of winter when everything is grey, try some of the alpine primulas. You'll need patience because they are slow growing, but once the plants are established, they put on a glorious show of flowers, with scarcely a leaf to be seen. Originally from the European Alps, alpine primulas (also known as European primulas) are usually found growing in cracks and crevices, where the water can drain away easily.

Most of the hybrids seen in cultivation originate from crosses between two of the wild species—*P.marginata* and *P. allionii*—but other species have also been introduced and subsequent hybridization makes it fairly difficult to ascertain which category they should fall under. Let's just say you are likely to come across so-called *P. ×pubescens* hybrids which are a cross between *P. auricula* and *P. hirsuta*. You will also find *P. ×loiseleurii* hybrids, which are cross between *P. allionii* and *P. auricula*.

Alpine primulas do well in troughs and rockeries and are perfect for scree gardens. Because they flower so early in the year, it's nice to have them under your eye close to the house for times when the weather is too bad to venture far into the garden

Primula 'Clarence Elliott'

The large lilac-mauve flowers have a white centre and wavy margins. The plant forms a cushion of typically *P. allionii* leaves. It is often seen on the show bench in the United Kingdom.

ZONES 3–9
HABIT AND SIZE Forms low rosettes up to 4 in. (10 cm). Stem height 3 in. (8 cm).
FLOWERING Early spring.
ORIGIN A cross between *P. allionii* and *P. marginata* 'Linda Pope' raised by Joe Elliott in 1982.
LANDSCAPE AND DESIGN USES Rockery, troughs, or pots.
SIMILAR PLANTS *Primula* 'Jo-Jo' has large blue-lilac flowers with a creamy yellow eye.

Primula 'Lee Myers'▲

Small bright pink, slightly ruffled flowers over neat rosettes of grey-green leaves. A vigorous grower.

ZONES 3–9
HABIT AND SIZE Forms a low, compact clump 4 × 5 in. (10 × 20 cm). Stem height 2 in. (5 cm).
FLOWERING Early to midspring.
ORIGIN A hybrid of *P. allionii* raised by British grower Len Bailey.
LANDSCAPE AND DESIGN USES Grows well in a rockery, trough, or pot.
SIMILAR PLANTS *Primula allionii* × *P.* 'White Linda Pope' has large clear pink flowers with a white eye. It is free flowering and was raised in England by Joe Elliott at his Broadwell nursery.

Primula ×loiseleurii 'Aire Mist'▼

This vigorous hybrid produces a cushion of bright white flowers above a dark green mound of foliage.

ZONES 3–9
HABIT AND SIZE Slow growing. Forms a low clump. Stem height less than 1 in. (2.5 cm).
FLOWERING Early to midspring.
ORIGIN Raised by Peter Lister in the United Kingdom from a cross between *P.* 'Blairside Yellow' and *P. allionii*.
LANDSCAPE AND DESIGN USES Grows well in a well-drained rockery, trough, or scree garden.
SIMILAR PLANTS *Primula ×loiseleurii* 'Aire Waves' is very similar except that the flowers have wavy petals and appear a few weeks earlier. *Primula* 'Snowcap' produces pure white flowers over a compact rosette of dark green slightly sticky leaves. *Primula* 'Tony' is a marginata hybrid with white flowers held on small stems.

Primula ×*loiseleurii* 'Lismore Yellow'

A strong-growing primula with numerous blooms of soft yellow held on short stems. Much sought after as the colour is uncommon in alpine primulas.

ZONES 3–9

HABIT AND SIZE Slow growing. Forms a low, compact clump 4 × 5 in. (10 × 20 cm). Stem height to 6 in. (15 cm).

FLOWERING Early to midspring.

ORIGIN A cross between *P. auricula* var. *ciliata* and some white clones of *P. allionii*. Raised by Brian and Judith Burrow in the United Kingdom in the 1970s and 1980s along with many other "Lismore" hybrids.

LANDSCAPE AND DESIGN USES Rockery, troughs, or pots.

SIMILAR PLANTS *Primula* 'Kath Dryden' has loose heads of very pale yellow flowers.

Primula marginata 'Barbara Clough'

An attractive plant with slightly toothed powdery leaves. The flowers are pinkish lilac with a white eye.

ZONES 3–9
HABIT AND SIZE Polyanthus form. Rosette forming. Stem height 4 in. (10 cm).
FLOWERING Early to midspring.
ORIGIN A selection of *P. marginata*.
LANDSCAPE AND DESIGN USES Grows well in a rockery, trough, or pot.
SIMILAR PLANTS *Primula marginata* 'Napoleon' has pale lavender flowers and strongly toothed leaves edged with farina.

Primula marginata 'Linda Pope'

Silver-edged primrose 'Linda Pope'

One of the best-known marginata hybrids with jagged silvery leaves and large pale mauve-blue flowers.

ZONES 3–9
HABIT AND SIZE Rosette forming. Stem height 6 in. (15 cm).
FLOWERING Late winter to early spring.
ORIGIN First mentioned in 1911. Raised by British nurseryman Mr Pope of Birmingham who named it after his daughter.
LANDSCAPE AND DESIGN USES Rockery, trough, or pot.
SIMILAR PLANTS *Primula ×pubescens* 'Wedgwood' has similar flowers and form, but its leaves aren't as striking.

Primula 'Pink Ice'

Large white flowers with pink-edged petals above small foliage rosettes.

ZONES 3–9
HABIT AND SIZE Slow growing. Forms a low, compact clump 4 × 5 in. (10 × 20 cm). Flowers are stemless.
FLOWERING Late winter to early spring.
ORIGIN From a cross between *P. allionii* and *P.* ×*pubescens* 'Harlow Carr' raised by Brian and Judith Burrow in the United Kingdom.
LANDSCAPE AND DESIGN USES Rockery, trough, or scree garden.
SIMILAR PLANTS *Primula* 'Lea Gardens' is another hybrid of *P. allionii* and its large white flowers have a pink tinge to the edge of the petals.

Primula ×pubescens 'Mrs J. H. Wilson'

Bright, light purple flowers with a white centre above finely toothed leaves. Very easy to grow.

ZONES 3–9
HABIT AND SIZE Slow growing. Forms a low, compact clump. Stem height 4 in. (10 cm).
FLOWERING Early to midspring.
ORIGIN An old variety that was mentioned by British plant explorer Reginald Farrer in 1914.
LANDSCAPE AND DESIGN USES Rockery, trough, or scree garden.
SIMILAR PLANTS *Primula ×pubescens* 'Boothman's Variety' is a vigorous and easy variety bearing dark reddish purple flowers with a small starry white eye.

Primula ×pubescens 'Wharfedale Ling'

Tight small rosettes of leathery green foliage are covered with small creamy white blooms with a prominent pink edge.

ZONES 3–9
HABIT AND SIZE Clump forming. Flowers are stemless.
FLOWERING Late winter to early spring.
ORIGIN All the plants in the Wharfedale series were bred by Alec Stubbs in the United Kingdom.
LANDSCAPE AND DESIGN USES Rockery, troughs, or pots.
SIMILAR PLANTS *Primula* 'Wharfedale Gem' has darker pink flowers with a white centre. *Primula* 'Wharfedale Superb' has white flowers edged with mauve.

Primula 'Rachel Kinnen'

A robust grower with large mauve-pink flowers.

ZONES 3–9
HABIT AND SIZE Forms large clumps. Flowers held on small stems above the foliage. Stem height 4 in. (10 cm).
FLOWERING Early to midspring.
ORIGIN A hybrid of unknown parents raised by Frank Shipston in the 1980s.
LANDSCAPE AND DESIGN USES Rockery, trough, or scree garden.
SIMILAR PLANTS *Primula allionii* 'Garnet Red' has dark pink flowers and bright green, lightly toothed leaves. *Primula* 'Hurstwood Midnight' is a lovely hybrid with dark velvety purple flowers and a star-shaped cream eye. The flowers are borne on slightly longer stems like an auricula.

AURICULAS

Auriculas are the aristocrats of the primula world. Also known as bear's ears (due to the shape of the leaf), they are fascinating plants grown for their beautiful, extremely varied, velvety flowers. Horticulturists have divided the many auriculas into several subgroups, including Border and Show. In general, the Border auriculas are grown for the open garden (in rockeries, stone troughs, or even a well-drained border) and are to be distinguished from the Show auriculas (generally grown in pots), which have been bred to exacting standards for centuries with a view to exhibiting the flowers or as part of a collection. However, even the Show auriculas, apart from a few tricky exceptions, are very easy to grow by the novice gardener.

All auriculas are very hardy garden plants that can withstand a lot of neglect and very cold temperatures. Every garden has a shady spot or an outside windowsill for a few auriculas. But be warned they are extremely addictive.

Primula auricula 'Brookfield'

This is a grey edge auricula although the classification into white and grey categories is somewhat hazy and depends on how much meal is on the petals. The amount of meal can vary with cultural conditions, but generally 'Brookfield' is classified as a grey-edge. It is an attractive and vigorous plant.

ZONES 3–9
HABIT AND SIZE Clump forming.
FLOWERING Mid to late spring.
CULTIVATION A fairly vigorous plant but may need some attention to obtain really good flowers.
ORIGIN Raised by Peter Ward in 1976.
LANDSCAPE AND DESIGN USES Pot culture under shelter from the rain.
SIMILAR PLANTS *Primula auricula* 'Maggie', a grey edge or white, is also a vigorous grower. It was raised by Allan Hawkes in 1966. *Primula auricula* 'Grey Lag', a grey edge on a black background, was raised by Jack Ballard around 1955.

Primula auricula 'Butterwick'

A gold-centred Alpine auricula in shades of rich brownish red.

ZONES 3–9
HABIT AND SIZE Clump forming.
FLOWERING Mid to late spring.
CULTIVATION An easy, vigorous plant.
ORIGIN Raised by Frank Jacques in 1979.
LANDSCAPE AND DESIGN USES Can be planted in the garden in a shady well-drained position but does well in containers.
SIMILAR PLANTS *Primula auricula* 'Piers Telford' has attractive flowers in orange-brown shades. It was raised by Derek Telford in 1991. *Primula auricula* 'Ancient Society' is another gold-centred Alpine in orangey shades, which is slightly lighter than 'Piers Telford'. It is named in honour of the Ancient Society of York Florists, the oldest gardening club, which dates back to 1768.

Primula auricula 'Everest Blue'

A blue Show Self auricula. These blue colours are some of the most stunning in this category. This one is a robust plant with lightly mealed foliage which offsets readily.

ZONES 3–9
HABIT AND SIZE Clump forming.
FLOWERING Mid to late spring.
CULTIVATION Easy.
ORIGIN Raised by Harold D. Hall in 1959 from seed obtained from auricula breeder C. G. Haysom.
LANDSCAPE AND DESIGN USES Because the farina, or paste, in the centre of the flower spoils in the rain, most people grow Selfs in a pot with some protection from the elements, such as in a cold conservatory or alpine house or on a protected windowsill.
SIMILAR PLANTS *Primula auricula* 'Remus', a reliable purple-blue, was raised by W. R. Hecker in the 1960s. *Primula auricula* 'Martin Luther King', also dark blue, is another firm favourite sometimes known as MLK.

Primula auricula
'Fiddler's Green'

This is a great plant for its novelty aspect but it is also a very vigorous and fairly easy variety to grow. It is a Double green-edge and is certainly unusual.

ZONES 3–9
HABIT AND SIZE Clump forming.
FLOWERING Mid to late spring.
CULTIVATION Usually quite vigorous and easy to grow but best kept in pots.
ORIGIN Introduced by Cherille Hebdon in 2001.
LANDSCAPE AND DESIGN USES Definitely a plant to keep in a visible spot as a talking piece.
SIMILAR PLANTS *Primula auricula* 'Sword', a Double green-edge, is very similar to 'Fiddler's Green' but with more doubling and slightly pointy petals. It doesn't offset as freely.

Primula auricula 'Fred Booley'

A beautiful lilac-blue Double auricula. Very floriferous and lightly fragrant.

ZONES 3–9
HABIT AND SIZE Clump forming.
FLOWERING Mid to late spring.
CULTIVATION Usually quite vigorous and easy to grow.
ORIGIN This cultivar was introduced in 1999 by Derek Salt, a prolific amateur breeder in Lincolnshire, England, who has produced many wonderful doubles and has made a significant contribution to their return to popularity. He is known for producing vigorous plants with slightly rounder leaves than other cultivars and very full doubling of the petals.
LANDSCAPE AND DESIGN USES Great garden or container plants. A big pot of Double auriculas is a stunning sight.
SIMILAR PLANTS Two other introductions raised by Derek Salt are *P. auricula* 'Lincoln Bullion', a bright yellow Double, and *P. auricula* 'Lincoln Chestnut', a mustardy coloured Double.

Primula auricula 'Greenpeace'

A Show Fancy auricula with a green edge and yellow body.

ZONES 3–9
HABIT AND SIZE Clump forming.
FLOWERING Mid to late spring.
CULTIVATION We find this cultivar to be a reliable and consistent flowerer, though that is not the case with all the plants in this category.
ORIGIN Raised by John Fielding.
LANDSCAPE AND DESIGN USES Most people grow Fancy auriculas in pots under protection, such as a cold frame or cold greenhouse, so the humidity and temperature levels can be controlled.
SIMILAR PLANTS *Primula auricula* 'Parakeet', a striking North American cultivar, is described as having irregular green edges and pointy petals, giving it a star-shaped appearance.

Primula auricula 'James Arnot'

This is a white edge Show auricula, as the green edge is covered with so much farina that the edge of the petals appear white. It also has attractive mealy foliage. It is a very popular plant that is regularly exhibited.

ZONES 3–9

HABIT AND SIZE Clump forming.

FLOWERING Mid to late spring.

CULTIVATION Not for the novice grower but not as tricky as some other white-edges.

ORIGIN Raised by Tom Meek in 1961.

LANDSCAPE AND DESIGN USES Most people grow white or grey auriculas in pots under protection, such as a cold frame or cold greenhouse, so the humidity and temperature levels can be controlled and so that the farina is not damaged by rain.

SIMILAR PLANTS *Primula auricula* 'C. G. Haysom', a reliable white-edge that has stood the test of time, has attractive serrated, mealy foliage and offsets freely. It was raised by R. Loake in 1962 and named after auricula grower C. G. Haysom, who bred many fine edge varieties from 1930 to the 1960s.

Primula auricula 'Lord Saye en Sele'

A Striped auricula. This particular variety has stripes of red, yellow, and green.

ZONES 3–9
HABIT AND SIZE Clump forming.
FLOWERING Mid to late spring.
CULTIVATION We have found the Stripes tend to be quite vigorous plants that freely produce offsets. 'Lord Saye en Sele' is a particularly easy variety to start with.
ORIGIN Bred by Alan Hawkes in 1987.
LANDSCAPE AND DESIGN USES Most people grow Show Fancy varieties in pots under protection, such as a cold frame or cold greenhouse, so the humidity and temperature levels can be controlled, but they can be grown in the garden in a well-drained position.
SIMILAR PLANTS *Primula auricula* 'Arundell', sometimes called 'Arundell Stripe', is a vigorous plant with red, white, and yellow stripes. It was raised by Ray Donard in 1986. *Primula auricula* 'Darent Tiger' is another easy plant with red and cream stripes. *Primula auricula* 'Königin der Nacht', a very striking cultivar, is dark purple with white stripes and powdery leaves. It was raised by Allan Guest in 1988.

Primula auricula 'Mikado'

This is a Show Self auricula with dark red to black flowers and non-mealy leaves.

ZONES 3–9
HABIT AND SIZE Clump forming.
FLOWERING Mid to late spring.
CULTIVATION Some Selfs need a bit of persuasion to produce good flowers and are not always as vigorous as the Alpines, but are worth the effort.
ORIGIN Raised by W. Smith in 1906.
LANDSCAPE AND DESIGN USES Because the farina, or paste, in the centre of the flower spoils in the rain, most people grow Selfs in a pot with some protection from the elements, such as in a cold conservatory or alpine house or on a protected windowsill.
SIMILAR PLANTS *Primula auricula* 'Wincha' is another very dark Self auricula which has an almost velvety appearance. It was raised by Tim Coop.

Primula auricula 'Mojave'

A lovely light red Show Self auricula with mealy foliage like most of the auriculas in this category.

ZONES 3–9
HABIT AND SIZE Clump forming.
FLOWERING Mid to late spring.
CULTIVATION Fairly easy cultivar.
ORIGIN Raised by English breeder Peter Ward and exhibited in 1980.
LANDSCAPE AND DESIGN USES Best grown with some shelter from the elements to avoid spoiling the farina.
SIMILAR PLANTS *Primula auricula* 'Favourite' is a good vigorous Show Self cultivar for the beginner. The flowers are bright red and the white centre is very neat. Raised by Ben Simonite in 1904, so it has stood the test of time.

Primula auricula 'Old Irish Blue'

This old Border auricula has frilly blue flowers shaded dark to light blue. Like most Borders, it is scented and the leaves are a non-mealy apple-green colour. Many plants available under this name are equally as lovely but may not be the true original plant. Pat FitzGerald Nurseries in Ireland is micro-propagating this plant, which may mean it will be more widely available in the future.

ZONES 3–9
HABIT AND SIZE It forms large clumps in the garden. Stem height 8 in. (20 cm) tall.
FLOWERING Mid to late spring.
CULTIVATION Border auriculas are some of the easiest to grow. They will do best in well-drained soil in a pot or border. A layer of gravel can be added around the neck of the plant to protect the leaves from excess moisture.
ORIGIN An old Irish variety that was shown at Chelsea Flower Show in the 1920s.
LANDSCAPE AND DESIGN USES Tradition has it that Border auriculas were often found lining the path leading up to the front door of Victorian terraced houses. However, they are great for rockeries and grow well under shrubs with late foliage such as smaller-growing roses or fuchsias. They are also showy flowers very suitable for containers and troughs which raise the flowers up to eye height.
SIMILAR PLANTS Plenty of blue seed-raised plants adapt perfectly well to the open garden, but here are two other old, named Border auriculas that continue to thrive. *Primula auricula* 'Blue Velvet', dark blue with a white eye, has bright green leaves devoid of meal and is highly scented. *Primula auricula* 'MacWatt's Blue' has rich purple-blue flowers with a large, well-farinated white eye and densely mealed leaves.

Primula auricula 'Prague'

A green edge Show auricula. This cultivar is often seen on the show bench and has a light green edge. The well-shaped flowers have a black background and a white powdery centre.

ZONES 3–9
HABIT AND SIZE Clump forming.
FLOWERING Mid to late spring.
CULTIVATION Some of the edge varieties can be quite tricky and flower unreliably, inconsistently, or not at all, but therein lies the challenge.
ORIGIN Raised by David Hadfield in 1976.
LANDSCAPE AND DESIGN USES Most people grow the edged auriculas in pots under protection, such as a cold frame or cold greenhouse, so the humidity and temperature levels can be controlled and the farina is not damaged by rain.
SIMILAR PLANTS *Primula auricula* 'Bob Lancashire' is another reliable green-edged auricula. *Primula auricula* 'Oban', an easy green edge, off-sets well and produces a nice flower without too much effort.

Primula auricula 'Rajah'

A Show Fancy auricula that produces lovely green edged flowers with a body of bright scarlet-red and a small paste centre.

ZONES 3–9
HABIT AND SIZE Clump forming.
FLOWERING Mid to late spring.
CULTIVATION An easy plant to grow, quite free flowering.
ORIGIN Originates from the House of Douglas, England, in the 1950s.
LANDSCAPE AND DESIGN USES Best grown under protection from excessive wet in a cool alpine house or on a windowsill.
SIMILAR PLANTS *Primula auricula* 'Astolat', a Show Fancy auricula that produces lovely green-edged flowers with a white centre and a pink body colour. The petals are usually quite pointed. Raised by W. R. Hecker around 1971. *Primula auricula* 'Rolts', another Fancy auricula with a red body and a green edge. A vigorous grower, it is an old cultivar raised by A. C. Rolt in 1894.

Primula auricula 'Sirius'

This is an Alpine auricula in the gold-centred category. The colours are quite difficult to describe, but the blooms are maroon-purple shaded to cream. This is one of our favourites as its colours are so unusual and they are also very bright and distinctive.

ZONES 3–9
HABIT AND SIZE Clump forming.
FLOWERING Mid to late spring.
CULTIVATION An easy, vigorous plant.
ORIGIN Raised by Frank Jacques in 1979.
LANDSCAPE AND DESIGN USES Can be planted in the garden in a shady well-drained position but also does well in containers.
SIMILAR PLANTS *Primula auricula* 'Lee Paul' was bred from 'Sirius' and is a gold-centred Alpine with maroon-brown petals shading to an antiqued orange-yellow. Raised by Derek Telford, 'Lee Paul' has won several prizes on the show bench.

Primula auricula 'Star Wars'

This is one of our favourites as it quite easy to grow and produces some stunning flowers. It has a grey edge and purple body. Traditionally, it would have been classed as a grey edge Show Fancy auricula because it hasn't got a black background and the petals can be slightly pointy.

ZONES 3–9
HABIT AND SIZE Clump forming.
FLOWERING Mid to late spring.
CULTIVATION Relatively easy to grow but other plants in this category may prove quite tricky.
ORIGIN Raised by Tim Coop.
LANDSCAPE AND DESIGN USES Most people grow Show Fancy varieties in pots under protection, such as a cold frame or cold greenhouse, so the humidity and temperature levels can be controlled.
SIMILAR PLANTS *Primula auricula* 'Hawkwood', a grey edge with a dark red body, is quite easy to grow.

Primula auricula 'The Baron'

A yellow Self auricula.

ZONES 3–9
HABIT AND SIZE Clump forming.
FLOWERING Mid to late spring.
CULTIVATION Vigorous and easy to grow.
ORIGIN Raised by J. Baxter in 1980.
LANDSCAPE AND DESIGN USES Best grown in pots.
SIMILAR PLANTS *Primula auricula* 'Brazil' is a good yellow with well-mealed foliage. It produces many offsets and was bred by Derek Telford in 1982. *Primula auricula* 'Pot o' Gold' is a bright yellow Self bred by Gwen Baker in 1983. It is a vigorous grower that flowers reliably.

Primula auricula 'Victoria de Wemyss'

This Alpine auricula has deep blue to light blue petals with a cream or white centre which puts it in the light-centred category. It is a stunning blue that can be quite breathtaking.

ZONES 3–9
HABIT AND SIZE Clump forming.
FLOWERING Mid to late spring.
CULTIVATION An easy, vigorous plant.
ORIGIN Raised by Jack Wemyss-Cooke in 1979.
LANDSCAPE AND DESIGN USES Can be planted in the garden in a shady, well-drained position but does well in containers.
SIMILAR PLANTS *Primula auricula* 'Adrian', raised by Arthur Delbridge in 1971, has bright purple to light purple-blue flowers. *Primula auricula* 'Walton', raised by Gordon Douglas in 1957, is a popular plant with white- or cream-centred blue to violet flowers.

GROWING
AND
PROPAGATING

P

Primulas are easy plants to grow as long as they are given the right conditions. When provided with sufficient moisture and shade, they thrive in many types of climates, gardens, and situations. They have the added benefit of being easily transplanted, so if they are not doing well where you have planted them you can just dig them up and try them somewhere else.

Hardiness and Climate

Most primulas hate cosseting, and the varieties mentioned in this book are among the most hardy, withstanding temperatures as low as -22°F (-30°C). Some of the best collections are found in the cool, moist regions of Scotland, Norway, and even Alaska, but it is possible to grow primulas well in areas that are less than ideal if you take care to provide the right planting and soil conditions.

All the primulas in this book are hardy throughout the British Isles, even in severe winters. There are also many successful growers of primulas in the United States and Canada, though obviously it is a challenge in some of the very warm southern states. The

Primula Pacific Giant hybrid (front left), *P. denticulata* hybrids (right and centre), *P.* 'Dorothy' (left), and *P. elatior* at the Jensen-Olson Arboretum in Alaska.

Pacific Northwest states of Oregon and Washington have a similar climate to the southwest of England and there are many growers in these areas. The Canadian province of British Columbia is also a good primrose area.

If you have severe winters with plenty of snow cover, primulas should survive since the snow protects them. Very harsh icy conditions with no snow are more dangerous, and it's best to cover the plants with spruce or other evergreen branches for protection. Many of the Asiatic species, which are used to severe winters, lose their leaves entirely in winter and so they are protected by the soil.

If you have very warm, dry summers, shade will be essential. We know of some growers in very hot summers who have installed drip watering systems in their borders to keep their primroses sufficiently moist.

The hardiness zones included in the plant descriptions are general guidelines. Some plants may well grow in warmer or colder areas than indicated according to the location and exposure of your garden.

Cultivation Considerations

Different types of primula have quite different needs, which we have detailed in the plant entries. Here we consider general guidelines for the ornamental groups in the plant description section.

GROWING PRIMROSES AND POLYANTHUS

In the right conditions, primroses and polyanthus will flower for two or three months in early to late spring. Many also flower again in the autumn before going dormant for the winter although the blooms may not be as prolific or even the same colour and size as the spring flowers.

Primroses and polyanthus will grow in almost any ordinary garden soil, but they grow best in a soil with a pH of 6.5–7.0, and generally do better in clay soil that is enriched with humus to help water retention in summer and drainage in winter. This can take the form of garden compost, leaf mould, well-rotted manure, spent mushroom compost, seaweed, and so on. In sandy soil, primulas are likely to last one season and not thrive. It is possible, however, to improve their longevity by adding as much humus as possible.

Primroses and polyanthus prefer a site in the garden with sun in the morning and protection from strong heat in the afternoon. In the wild, they are found in open, deciduous woodland or on north-facing slopes and sheltered banks. In a garden, a site under dappled shade works very well. The plants tolerate full sun if the soil is well enriched with organic matter and if nearby plants shade them in midsummer. They will also grow in shade. In fact, in full shade, they often have a longer flowering season but the full richness of the colours might be sacrificed.

If given enough moisture, primroses and polyanthus reward those who grow them by bulking up and flowering beautifully. However, they do not tolerate being waterlogged, so the soil needs to be free draining. When planting underneath mature trees or hedges, bear in mind that a large area of soil can be parched by the roots, so be careful not to plant primroses too close to these larger plants. Once established in the garden, primrose and polyanthus should not need watering, unless in a very exposed situation in the summer. Reduce the need for watering

Primula vulgaris Kennedy hybrids in a border at Blarney Castle.

How to Improve Your Soil

ADDING SOIL IMPROVERS to poor soil transforms the performance of all primulas. These amendments can be dug into the soil before planting or used as annual mulch, and they don't have to cost a fortune. If you don't already have one, make a compost heap, or rather two or three. Having a succession of piles seems to work better. Leaf mould is easy to make. Just put the leaves in plastic sacks, preferably when they're a bit damp, make some holes in the side of the sack, and set the sacks out of sight for about a year. If you live near a beach, mixing seaweed into the soil adds useful minerals to it. Even if you live in a town, there are often places where you might be able to beg some stable manure. It is vital, however, only to use well-rotted manure—whether from horses, cows, or chickens. The manure shouldn't smell at that stage and it won't burn the plants. Spent mushroom compost is sometimes also available and adds useful organic matter.

by providing a good mulch of leaf mould, garden compost, or the like, to help retain the moisture.

Gardeners in climates where temperatures often exceed 86°F (30°C) in the summer and do not become cold in winter may have trouble growing many primroses and polyanthus. One reason for this is because the plants need winter chill and will suffer in the heat unless grown in a very shady and moist environment. In regions where temperatures fall below -4°F (-20°C), it is recommended that plants be covered in winter with conifer branches or other suitable material unless they get a good covering of snow.

To keep primroses vigorous, they should be lifted and divided every few years. Otherwise, they tend to dwindle away. Although this may seem like a lot of work, it is also a chance to produce more plants for your garden or to share with friends. Most of the hardy primrose and polyanthus varieties set seed if grown in groups. Insects cross-pollinate the plants, so if the weather is too cold and there are not many insects about, you may not get much viable seed. Most primrose and polyanthus can hybridize with each other, but the seed that is produced is rarely true to the parent. Even if you only have one type of primula in your garden, the bees may visit your neighbours, which is why you can end up with different coloured seedlings in your garden.

GROWING DOUBLE PRIMROSES

Double primroses flower from very early to late spring, depending on the variety, and are hardy in zones 4–8. Although they tolerate very cold conditions if they have a protective layer of snow, they may need some extra cover to help them through the winter in areas where the temperature descends below -4°F (-20°C), especially if subjected to alternate freezing and thawing. Some spruce boughs or something similar should do the trick.

The plants appreciate a site in dappled shade. They don't like being waterlogged, so soil should be enriched with as much organic matter as possible to increase drainage and to provide food for the plant. Double primroses need more nourishment than most other primulas.

Because double primroses don't carry seed, they make up for it by trying to flower as much as possible, sometimes more than 100 blossoms at a time. Regular division of the plants is therefore essential to restore their vigour. Picking posies of double flowers helps a plant to avoid exhausting itself.

You can try raising double primroses from seed. The proportion of double flowers from a packet would be about 25 percent, but these doubles would be your own unique, never-seen-before plants.

Double primroses 'Guernsey Cream' and 'Petticoat'

GROWING JULIANA PRIMROSES

Juliana primroses bloom from midwinter to early spring and are hardy in zones 4–8. The stoloniferous (creeping) roots mean that the plant spreads easily and lends itself particularly well to propagation by division. The flowers are acaulis form or small stalked polyanthus or a mixture of both.

The plants need a damp, but well-drained soil. If you add plenty of organic matter to the soil, Julianas will reward you by multiplying readily. A good mulch of leaf mould in spring and autumn will conserve water and protect the roots in winter. Dappled shade is best but Julianas tolerate more sun than some of the other acaulis primroses and polyanthus if grown in a damp place. Try to avoid afternoon sun.

To keep plants vigorous, divide them every couple of years or so in the autumn or early spring.

In Jack-in-the-Green forms the flower is surrounded by a large ruff of green leaves.

GROWING UNUSUAL FORMS

Unusual forms flower from late winter to midspring and are hardy in zones 4–9. They are no more difficult to cultivate than any of the "usual" forms such as primroses and polyanthus and are often extremely floriferous. Bear in mind that these are hybrids and any seed they produce is unlikely to have a very high percentage of unusual forms, so it is best to split them regularly to keep them going.

The soil needs to be damp, but also well drained, not always an easy combination. Both of these conditions can be helped by adding lots of organic matter such as well-rotted manure, leaf mould, or mushroom compost. Dappled shade is ideal or a position that doesn't get the strong afternoon sun.

These oddities are best divided about every two years, or when the clump is getting very big.

GROWING CANDELABRAS

Candelabras extend the primula season. The first of them, usually the hybrids and cultivars of *Primula japonica*, begin flowering in late spring, and it is possible to have a succession of bloom right up until the end of summer. Most of the species in this group lose their leaves in winter and die back to a resting bud. This means they do well in very cold weather especially where there is plenty of snow cover.

Many candelabras have long root systems, so it pays to dig deeply when preparing the soil for planting. The ideal soil is a heavy acidic one, well enriched with organic matter to

Candelabra primulas in the bog garden at Furzey Gardens, Minstead, England.

avoid summer dryness. The plants prefer a site in dappled shade but can be planted in full sun if the site is moist and doesn't dry out in summer. Some of the red candelabras can be bleached by too much sun.

This group needs a lot of water in the growing months of spring and summer. If the plants dry out completely in summer, they will not survive. In their natural habitat, these species don't have a lot of moisture in the winter when they are dormant as the ground is usually frozen, so it's a mistake to think that because they are described as bog garden plants they will tolerate very wet conditions year-round. The idea is to keep them dry in winter but give them plenty of moisture in the growing period. This is fairly easy to achieve in areas with very cold winters by growing the plants in a ditch that is dry in winter and then is a run-off in the spring for melting snow. In places with mild winters and abundant rainfall, try to ensure that the bed is very well drained by adding lots of grit and humus at planting time. Avoid planting in areas that will be flooded, otherwise the roots

Candelabras grow well in this natural ditch garden in Ontario, Canada, which becomes a stream during spring runoff and after heavy rains. The soil is heavy wet clay.

will just rot. For example, if planting next to a stream, you could dam the beds in winter and open them again in the spring.

Candelabras can be divided every couple of years in autumn or early spring but this is not as necessary as with some of the other primulas. The plants can be left to proliferate for several years. They also self-seed, so be careful with the hoe or collect the ripe seed and scatter it in other places in the garden.

GROWING BELLED PRIMULAS

Belled primulas bloom from late spring to midsummer, with some species continuing until early autumn. They vary in height from 4 in. to 4 ft. (10–120 cm) and will form clumps about 8 in. (20 cm) across. Like other primulas in this book, they are hardy in zones 3–9.

Often they are grouped with candelabras as bog garden primulas because they like similar growing conditions: a rich, damp soil and partial shade. In the wild, they grow in damp meadows and by streamsides where they have abundant moisture during the flowering season. In the garden, they mustn't be allowed to dry out in summer. Light, dappled shade is ideal, but they will tolerate full sun if conditions are very damp.

Most varieties will self-seed, but can also be propagated by division.

Primula florindae in a shady garden in Ontario, Canada.

GROWING *PRIMULA SIEBOLDII*

Primula sieboldii is a creeping, deciduous species with stems 9–12 in. (22–30 cm) tall. Its leaves disappear very early in late summer to protect the plants from dry conditions and from the cold of winter, reappearing in late spring. The species and its hybrids flower from late spring to early summer and are hardy in zones 4–8, reportedly even as low as zone 3. As woodland plants they thrive best in dappled shade, but any other shady position in the garden will do. Some of the varieties have very long stems so avoid windy or exposed sites.

The plants appreciate a rich, well-drained, acidic soil so make sure you prepare the beds well with added compost or well-rotted leaf mould. This group of plants does not tolerate lime-rich (chalky, alkaline) soil, so if they are not proliferating in your garden, it may be worth checking soil acidity. Mulch helps retain moisture and cover the roots, which tend to emerge from the soil and become exposed. Mulching recreates the same conditions as being covered by a new layer of soil after the snow melts.

Primula sieboldii likes moist sites in the growing period and should never be allowed to dry out completely or become completely waterlogged. Because the plants die down in summer soon after flowering, they seem to do well in warmer areas and thus are more widely grown in the United States than some of the other species, maybe because of their capacity to cope with more intense heat and cold winters because of the long dormant period. Just remember to mark where they are planted to avoid digging them up in the autumn when the leaves have disappeared.

These plants are very easy to divide but can be left in the ground without disturbance. They have a very distinct root system that will simply pull apart when dormant. They rarely set seed unless grown in mixed groups in the garden and some, such as the blue strains, rarely set seed naturally in cultivation and need to be divided. Seed is available from specialist companies.

Primula sieboldii flourishes in the dry shade bed at Carolyn's Shade Garden in Pennsylvania.

Primula marginata growing in tufa rock in the Alpine House at Kew Gardens.

GROWING ALPINE PRIMULAS

Alpine primulas flower from late winter to early spring and are hardy in zones 3–9. They can be grown outside in a rock garden, trough, or scree garden where alpine conditions are mimicked. They also work wonderfully well in shallow terracotta containers placed on a low garden wall or outside table. If you want to grow them for showing, then you will need to protect them in an alpine house or greenhouse.

The plants need a gritty, well-drained soil with some humus to help retain moisture in the summer. They intensely dislike too much wet and are better watered from below if possible, just enough to keep them growing, and very little in winter. If the cushion of leaves gets too sodden, it rots. A mulch of grit around the plant helps keep water away from its neck.

Alpines prefer a site in semishade but tolerate a sunny position as long as their roots stay cool. They also tolerate very cold conditions but only where there is protective snow cover; otherwise they may need some protection from excessive moisture in the winter months.

Plants are slow to germinate from seed, but are easily divided after flowering by gently pulling the plants apart. Water well after re-potting, then leave them until almost dry before watering again.

GROWING AURICULAS

Auriculas flower from mid to late spring and are hardy in zones 3–9. The length of the flowering period varies according to the temperatures in which the plants are grown. If the climate is too hot, plants may flower only very briefly, but in the right conditions the flowers usually last for three months and many plants flower again in the autumn. Please keep in mind that although these plants are tolerant of very cold conditions and do not need protection from frost, they dislike humid soil in winter. They also suffer in high heat, so a shady site is vital.

Border auriculas thrive in any reasonable well-draining garden soil and appreciate regular feeding (with tomato fertilizer, for example). They will repay you for adding extra organic matter into the soil such as well-rotted manure, but are not too fussy about soil. The most important aspect of growing them is drainage. If water is allowed to stagnate around the collar of the plants, they will rot, yet the soil must also stay slightly moist in summer. Try to keep wet leaves from settling on the plants in autumn. Auriculas in the garden shouldn't need watering except when they've just been planted, unless your particular weather conditions dictate. Auriculas can stand more sun than many other groups of primulas because they are alpine plants, but always do better in dappled shade.

Show auriculas are usually grown in alpine houses or greenhouses for protection from the elements that might spoil the perfection of the flower, but they can also be grown on outside windowsills or on shelving on north- or east-facing walls. The compost mixture for potted Show auriculas is a matter of great debate and discussion. Every grower seems to have his or her own recipe. We use an open fibrous compost with some perlite or vermiculite plus horticultural grit to improve drainage. It helps to experiment and see what works best for you, depending on what materials you have available.

For potted auriculas, getting the watering right is probably the most difficult part of their culture. Auriculas hate being waterlogged, but neither must they get dust dry. You are far more likely to kill them by overwatering than by underwatering. The plants need moist growing conditions and good drainage is the absolute key.

Auriculas may need dividing every couple of years when the older tissue in the middle dies down. If left undivided, plants tend to produce long carroty roots which protrude from the soil. They produce offsets off the main stem of the plant which makes them very easy to divide and is an easy way of sharing plants with friends or swopping plants with other collectors.

Border auriculas in an old ceramic sink.

Purchasing Plants and Seed

With thousands of primulas on the market, in local garden centres, and even at your local supermarket, you may have a hard time determining which primroses are hardy, which are not, and which should be treated as annuals. If you are buying in your local garden centre, unless you really want something that you wish to discard after a few weeks, check the hardiness ratings on the label and whether the plant is being marketed in the perennial section or not. If a plant is being kept under protection from the frost in a heated area of the shop, chances are it won't do well in the garden. Please note that hardy perennial primroses are usually more expensive than the spring annuals but you are investing in something that will give a lot of pleasure in years to come.

We also warn you not to buy primula seed that is on display in warm shops. If stored over a certain temperature, primula seed will no longer be viable and you will get very poor germination.

If you want to be sure you are buying correctly labelled hardy primula, we would suggest you buy from a reputable nursery. With more and more specialist nurseries shipping plants, it is getting easier to source that elusive plant you can't find anywhere else.

When to Plant

You can plant pot-grown primulas any time the ground is not frozen. Ideally, autumn is a good time because the plants will get established before the winter and then you will make the most of the entire flowering season. Most primulas have long roots so make a hole plenty big enough and make sure to break up the subsoil, adding organic matter. Plant 6–9 in. (15–25 cm) apart for most of the species, leaving a bigger gap of up to 20 in. (50 cm) for some of the larger Asiatic species such as the candelabras. The general rule is to not plant any deeper than the crown of the plant—that is, with the soil at the same level as it was in the pot—and press the soil down firmly but gently. Water plants in, even if it is about to rain, as that will avoid air pockets forming around the roots.

Ongoing Maintenance

In years gone by, gardeners would dig up primroses at the end of spring and replant them in the shade for the summer. Few of us can permit this luxury now, but we need to try and reproduce wild growing conditions as far as possible. When planted under small shrubs, roses, and the like, primulas receive the shade they need after flowering and are protected from too much sun. A good mulch of organic matter around them helps to keep in moisture and feeds the plants, particularly in summer, which is when they are vulnerable to drought.

Unless you intend to harvest seed for your own use, it helps plants keep their vigour if you cut off dead stems. This prevents the plants from setting seed and enables them to put all their energy into making new growth.

Do keep an eye out for pests, particularly when growing plants in pots or in a greenhouse. Early action in dealing with problems can often prevent catastrophe.

Most primulas do not need lots of extra fertilizer but extract all the nutrients they need from organic matter or well-rotted manure. If you do feed them, do so sparingly. Fertilizer that is too high in nitrogen will produce much soft growth which is very vulnerable to frost, and also produces cabbage-like leaves at the expense of flowers. Wood ash from a bonfire or woodburning stove is useful around primulas as the potash helps bloom colour and charcoal sweetens the soil. Double primroses may need a little extra in the way of nourishment as they produce so many flowers. Auriculas can benefit from a small amount of tomato feed from the time the buds start to appear until flowering.

Care of Container Plants

Primulas in containers need regular watering. It's best to give them a good soaking when they are dry rather than a frequent sprinkling. This encourages the deeper roots rather than ones just below the surface which can be more affected by the wind and the sun. It is essential that containers have good drainage so the excess water quickly runs off. Plants won't do well if they are kept soaking wet all the time, so definitely no saucers underneath to retain water. It helps to put some broken terracotta in the bottom of a container at planting time.

A mulch around the plants can look attractive, help retain moisture, and repel weeds, but keep an eye out for slugs, which can hide in mulch. We've found that rubbing petroleum jelly (Vaseline) round the rim of the container deters slugs and is not visible.

Regular cutting of spent flowers and stems encourages the plants to put out new ones, and it is essential to pick posies of double primroses to keep plants from exhausting themselves.

In winter, avoid letting dead leaves stay on the containers as they can cause rot, particularly with auriculas or alpine plants. Frost shouldn't be a problem unless the temperature falls below -4°F (-20°C) when you would need to use some protective covering.

In autumn or spring either change the compost in your container or refresh it by emoving as much old compost as possible then top up with a fresh mixture containing a slow-release fertilizer such as seaweed or blood, fish, and bone.

Pests and Diseases

Primulas are relatively trouble free, and when planted in the right place in the right soil they should not cause you too much anxiety. Healthy, well-grown plants are less susceptible to attack by pests or disease. Nevertheless, be alert for early signs of any possible problems so you can tackle them as they arise. It can be more tricky if raising plants in a greenhouse or alpine house as problems can multiply with alarming rapidity when your back is turned.

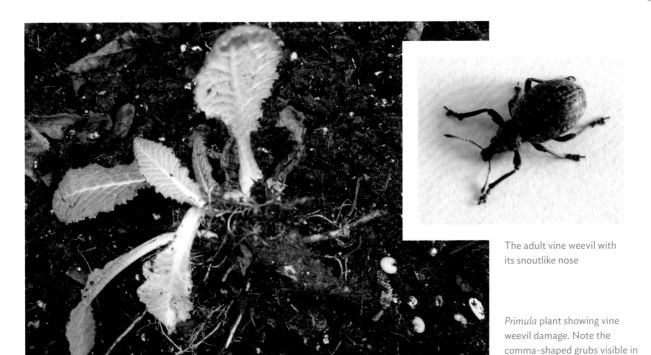

The adult vine weevil with its snoutlike nose

Primula plant showing vine weevil damage. Note the comma-shaped grubs visible in the soil surrounding the roots.

VINE WEEVIL

A real menace and probably the most important pest to look out for, particularly in potted plants, is the vine weevil. The adult is almost black and about ⅔ in. (2 cm) long. It emerges in autumn, looking like a beetle, but with the snout of a weevil. If you detect irregular notches eaten out of the sides of leaves, vine weevils may be present.

This pest is difficult to catch as it mainly comes out at night to feed, but it can be trapped by providing hiding places for it such as small rolls of corrugated cardboard that should be regularly checked and discarded. In greenhouses, check under pots or on the underside of benches where pests hide during the day.

In its juvenile stage, the vine weevil is a creamy comma-shaped grub with a brown head. About ⅓ in. (1 cm) long, the grub lives in the soil and has a particular liking for *Primula* roots. The grubs are the main problem. Normally, the first sign of their presence is the collapse of a plant which was perfectly healthy until then. When you tug on the plant, it lifts right out of the soil and has very few roots. The grubs are usually quite visible. If the plant is growing in a pot, simply remove the plant, squash the little beasties and get rid of the infected compost. Rinse off the plant roots and re-pot in some clean compost. Plants should recover well.

As a preventative measure, it is best to repot containers with clean compost every couple of years. Gravel around the neck of plants may also deter adult vine weevils from laying eggs, and anything which confuses their sense of smell may also help such as garlic sprays. If you have a larger infestation, you can treat your pots with specific nematodes (*Steinernema kraussel*), a biological control which is now widely available to the public. It is best to apply such a treatment twice a year as a drench in mid to late spring and again in late summer to early autumn. Bear in mind that nematodes are only active when the soil temperature is between 41°F and 68°F (5°C–20°C) and the soil needs to be damp.

Vine weevils are not normally a big problem in open ground, where they have natural predators such as birds, frogs, toads, and hedgehogs. Watering pathways and areas between plants with a weak solution of disinfectant, some crushed mothballs scattered in the area, or perhaps sowing chives or garlic between plants can help to discourage the adults. If you do start finding a lot of damage, it may be necessary to treat the patch with nematodes, though bear in mind that they give poor results in heavy or dry soils.

WHITEFLY AND GREENFLY

Whitefly and greenfly rarely are a problem in the garden but can cause problems in plants grown under glass as these pests spread rapidly. They often appear in early spring, causing unsightly white blotches to the leaves. The main worry is that they can spread virus. If tackled early, these pests can be controlled by spraying plants with an insecticidal soap.

ROOT APHID

Root aphids, also known as woolly aphids, can infest primulas in late summer, weakening the plants and introducing viruses. Again, this is mainly a problem in pot-grown plants, and auriculas are particularly susceptible. You will see fluffy white insects around the neck or roots of the plant, which, if not dealt with, can lead to sickly plants, stunted growth, and eventually the death of the plant. Keeping the plants cool and moist is an important part of prevention. Controls include keeping the primulas weed-free, as companion weeds also act as hosts to the aphids; not allowing primulas to dry out; and not reusing old potting compost. The only thing that seems to get rid of a bad infestation is to clean the compost off the roots, drench them in an appropriate oil-based insecticide, and repot.

RED SPIDER MITE

Again, mostly only a problem in the greenhouse where the conditions are too hot, red spider mite occasionally attacks plants grown in the garden, especially in pots. This pest is not actually a spider, but rather a tiny mite

White fly damage on leaves.

Root aphid around the neck of an infected plant.

Red spider damage on leaves.

that makes little white webs on the underside of leaves. It thrives in hot, dry conditions toward the end of the summer. The presence of mites on a plant can be detected by observing the leaves turn a mottled yellow or even white as the sap is sucked from them. Auriculas seem to be particularly vulnerable.

Red spider mite is not easy to get rid of once it has taken a hold, but there are various remedies such as spraying with neem oil or a nicotine solution. Predatory mites such as *Phytoseiulus persimilis* are now also available, but the temperature needs to be above 68°F (20°C) for them to thrive. The best control is obviously to avoid the infestation in the first place by not letting the plants dry out, and spraying the undersides of leaves. You could also ensure plants in pots are moved to a cool shady position over the summer months.

SLUGS AND SNAILS

Slugs can devour a tray of young seedlings and damage new growth in spring. Try sharp gravel, beer traps, wood ash, or other appropriate slug control. Slugs rarely destroy established plants completely but do certainly make them look less attractive. Another way to control slugs is to go out at night with a torch and a bucket and pick the pests off your plants. Your neighbours might think you are a little crazy, but it is certainly effective to remove slugs by hand. If you feel you need to use slug pellets, choose organic ones that cannot harm animals.

Caterpillar damage on leaves.

CATERPILLARS

The caterpillars of several moth and butterfly species can cause leaf and petal damage. They sometimes hollow out buds and eat seed heads. On established plants, the harm done is not usually terminal. Pick caterpillars off if you can see them; otherwise use an appropriate natural insecticide.

BIRDS

We definitely can't call them a pest, but sometimes they can be a nuisance, literally stripping the petals from the sweet-tasting flowers. If this is a serious problem, try stretching some black cotton thread over the area. It's not very noticeable to people but is dissuasive to the birds.

DEER, RABBITS, MICE, AND VOLES

Although they often leave primroses alone, rabbits may eat primroses when the leaves are at their most tender state, usually in early spring. You will usually see stems and flowers clipped off at a precise, 45° angle from the ground. Rabbits do not eat anything higher than about 2 feet (60 cm) off the ground so check surrounding plants to see whether there is higher damage. If there is, then deer could be the culprits. In that case, check for jagged broken stems and leaves where their blunt teeth have torn them away. If it is of any reassurance, primroses aren't usually the deer's favourite food.

Mice don't tend to be a particular problem though they are rather partial to the seed heads so keep a look out for them if you want to save the seed and get there first. Voles and moles can sometimes be a nuisance, tunnelling under beds and disturbing roots but do not usually cause uncontrolled damage.

FUNGUS

Botrytis, or grey mould, is the major fungal enemy of primulas but usually only a problem if plants are grown under glass. Good air circulation and the avoidance of overwatering or waterlogging in cold winter conditions are very important. Keep greenhouse plants well spaced and well ventilated during the winter months, and remove dead or dying leaves which may harbor fungus spores. Water very sparingly and then only from the bottom. If fungus has taken hold, remove all of the affected leaves and spray with an appropriate fungicide.

VIRUSES

Most viruses are transmitted by aphids or other sucking insects such as leafhoppers so if you keep those pests under control you shouldn't have a problem with viruses. Cucumber mosaic virus most commonly affects primroses and polyanthus. Telltale signs are stunted or distorted foliage. Don't panic straight away though as leaves are sometimes distorted by wind, frost damage, or even irregular watering. Check the new leaves as they come through. If they are distorted too, the whole plant should be destroyed, if possible by burning. Do not compost the plants.

Leaves showing the telltale furry signs of botrytis.

Distorted leaves may be a sign of virus.

Propagation

This is the fun bit. Planting the odd primula here and there in your garden doesn't do them justice. These plants are social creatures and best enjoyed en masse. The most economical way to achieve that is by propagating them yourself. Most primulas can be easily propagated either by division or seed sowing.

The British native primrose, *Primula vulgaris*, reproduces itself readily without any work on our part. Leave a few plants in a corner of your garden, treat the area to some neglect, and in a short time primroses will abound. Species such as *P. juliae* and *P. sieboldii* have a creeping rootstock and also spread themselves easily. The majority of hybrids, such as the polyanthus, however, need to be divided to be sure of getting more plants that are identical to the parent plant. Sometimes insects will do their work, resulting in new baby plants, but rarely are these identical to the mother plant.

Certain species throw their seed around with wild abandon, such as the candelabras and *Primula florindae*. They carry an abundance of seed high on the stem and if you are not too ready with the hoe around these plants and if the plants are growing in good conditions, you will see a host of small seedlings coming up which will quickly increase your stock. If they've been mixing with each other, you may have to root out any that have less desirable colours.

The only way to reproduce named plants, such as Show auriculas or named double primroses, is by division. Any seed collected from a named plant will not produce that exact same plant when it is sown.

Primula vulgaris hybridizes with other coloured primroses, creating a lovely mix of variously coloured self-seeded plants.

The Award of Garden Merit

THE ROYAL HORTICULTURAL SOCIETY'S Award of Garden Merit helps gardeners make informed choices about plants. This award indicates that the plant is recommended by the RHS as a reliable plant in the garden as a result of trial growings. It takes into consideration their all-round performance in the garden, availability, constitution, stability of colour and forms, and resistance to pests and diseases. Here is a nonexhaustive list of primulas that have been awarded the AGM.

Primula acaulis Danova Series
Primula alpicola
Primula auricula
Primula beesiana
Primula Barnhaven Blues Group
Primula bulleyana
Primula chionantha
Primula 'Clarence Elliott'
Primula cockburniana
Primula Crescendo Series
Primula denticulata
Primula elatior
Primula florindae
Primula 'Guinevere'
Primula 'Inverewe'
Primula japonica 'Miller's Crimson'
Primula japonica 'Postford White'
Primula 'Lady Greer'

Primula ×loiseleurii 'Aire Mist'
Primula marginata
Primula marginata 'Linda Pope'
Primula 'Marie Crousse'
Primula prolifera
Primula ×pubescens
Primula pulverulenta
Primula pulverulenta Bartley hybrids
Primula Rainbow Series
Primula rosea
Primula sieboldii
Primula sikkimensis
Primula 'Tony'
Primula veris
Primula vialii
Primula vulgaris
Primula 'Wanda'

Primula sieboldii is the ultimate
plant for any shade garden.

DIVISION

Primulas are perennial plants and in the right garden conditions give a good display for several seasons. However, very large clumps formed after two years of flowering benefit from being lifted and divided. All primulas appreciate being divided from time to time. It gets rid of old rootstock and encourages the plant to make new growth.

Dividing Primroses and Polyanthus

It's usually easy to see when primroses and polyanthus need dividing as they make very large clumps and can sometimes start to look a bit tired. For some of them, such as double primroses, dividing each year is highly recommended because the plants can exhaust themselves by carrying an abundance of flowers.

Primroses and polyanthus can be divided either immediately after flowering or in early autumn. Dividing in late spring has the advantage of giving a longer growing season, but exposes the divisions to the stress of summer heat and drought when they are most vulnerable. We usually divide in late summer and early autumn, and find that the plants are fully established, flowering freely the following spring. However, if your winters are particularly severe, you will probably get better results by dividing in late spring.

Lift the plant with a fork, taking enough soil to avoid damaging the roots. Shake off as much soil as possible, washing it off if necessary. Tease the roots apart and cut out large well-rooted crowns for replanting. Plant the small pieces too—you will probably be lucky! Discard the old woody centre of the plant. Before planting, trim the roots on the separated pieces back to about 4 in. (10 cm) and trim the leaves to the same length to prevent water loss during the early life of the separated plant. It's a good idea to soak the new pieces in clean cold water for a couple of hours before planting so that they will be plumped-up with water at replanting. Water in the new plantings with a half-strength potash solution and keep them moist and shaded until they are established.

Using a clean, sharp knife, cut off a thin slice of the rootball.

Carefully tease clumps apart to reveal separate plants.

Trim the leaves on separated plants back to about 4 in. (10 cm).

Remove excess soil from the roots using a clean fork.

Trim the roots on the separated plants back to about 4 in. (10 cm).

Pot up the new plants or replant directly in the garden.

Dividing Auriculas

If left to themselves in the garden, auriculas grow into glorious large clumps and only need to be divided if they start looking messy, with a lot of bare root (or carrot) showing above the ground (or if your friends are begging for a piece). Many experts recommend dividing after flowering, but in practice, the best time to divide is whenever you have the time to do it, as long as it is not too hot. Auriculas are even easier to separate than primroses. Just lift the clump and gently pull into separate plants, using a fork if necessary. Replant, making sure you water them well.

Auriculas grown in pots should be repotted every couple of years. However, at the nursery, we've had some huge pots of auriculas that we have left alone for years, intending each year to repot them, and then spring comes along and they are absolutely glorious—again. However, if potted auriculas are ignored for too long, they can get leggy and you must always be on the lookout for the dreaded vine weevil, which especially likes auricula roots in containers.

Show auriculas are often cultivated in small pots, but are generally divided more frequently than border (garden) ones. Auriculas produce offsets which grow from the main root. As long as they have roots, these offsets can be removed and potted up in a standard peat compost with a little sharp grit for drainage. Water in well and then keep cool and slightly on the dry side until established. Don't be tempted to overpot. Too large a pot means that the compost can become stale and waterlogged.

Auriculas that need dividing.

Cut the bare root ("carrot") with a clean knife.

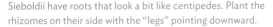

Sieboldii have roots that look a bit like centipedes. Plant the rhizomes on their side with the "legs" pointing downward.

Close-up of sieboldii roots.

Dividing *Primula sieboldii*

Primula sieboldii and hybrids should be lifted every three or four years when the foliage dies down in autumn. Tease apart the rhizomes, discarding the old centre of the plant, and selecting the younger outer ones for replanting. As the best flowers come after two years, it is recommended that you renew only a third of your plants each year.

Plant in a wide shallow hole with the roots spread out around the bud, and cover with about 1 in. (2.5 cm) of non-alkaline soil. Mark the spot where the rhizome is planted and wait for the new growth, which will not start until midspring or late spring the following year.

Dividing Candelabras and Belled Primula

Candelabra primulas can be divided every couple of years, preferably in the spring. They have fleshy long roots and you may need to use the back-to-back two-fork method to prise them apart.

Dividing Alpines

Primula allionii, *P. marginata*, and their hybrids are slow growing, so don't be too hasty in splitting them. If eventually you want to produce more plants, it is easy to pull a plant apart. This is best done in late spring, after flowering.

Finally, on a note of reassurance, in the nursery we find ourselves dividing whenever we have the time, no matter the time of year, even sometimes when plants are in flower. Primulas are forgiving plants.

SEED SOWING

The most economical way to produce lots of primulas for your garden is to sow from seed. It's not quite as easy as sowing mustard and cress, but following the right advice it works and is so, so satisfying. Unfortunately, just sprinkling seed in a flower bed as you might with annuals is not very effective, and you will achieve much more success by sowing in seed trays.

You can buy seeds from a reputable company or try keeping some of your own seed. If you collect your own seed, make sure you wait until the seeds are ripe—they will turn brown and the top of the capsule will open when they are ready. Then either sow them straight away or let them dry by hanging them in a paper bag for a week or two, shake them out of the capsules, and store in the fridge.

If you don't want to sow commercially obtained seeds when you receive them, put the packets in a screw-topped jar and store the jar in the fridge—not the freezer—until you are ready to plant. The seed can remain viable for several years. If you keep seed in a warm place, germination will be adversely affected.

The choice to sow in autumn or spring is yours. Opinions vary. At our nursery, we sow the majority of our seed between late winter and midspring. A little frost can aid germination, but in areas with very severe weather conditions you should delay sowing to midspring. You can sow later than this, but the later you leave it, the more difficult it is to bring small plants which are not well established through a winter season. Sieboldii primroses are best sown from mid autumn to mid winter. Most of the botanical species need natural freezing and thawing to get them started, so it's important to sow those as early as possible.

We have heard of endless methods of growing primula from seed and therefore we've come to the conclusion that there must be many ways that succeed. If you already have a method that works for you, stick with it. For those who have never tried, or never succeeded, here is what we do.

Use standard seed trays, or any suitable container with drainage holes. Fill the trays with compost. Where sowings of primula don't succeed, the main culprit is nearly always the compost. It needs to be a seed compost which is gritty and fibrous and containing very little fertilizer. Primula roots need air to grow and develop, and if the compost is too fine, a few waterings will drive all the air out.

Water the compost well after filling the trays, then sow seed on the surface. Do not cover the seed with soil. Very fine seeds can be sown on a layer of vermiculite or very fine gravel over the compost. Place a perforated seed tray of the same size over your sowings to protect the seed from birds and neighbourhood cats. Weigh the cover down with a stone.

Sow lightly on the surface of the compost.

Cover the seed trays to avoid disturbance of the soil.

Leave the covered trays in a shady place outdoors, making sure that you inspect them regularly and water as necessary. Drying out, especially as the seeds are on the point of germinating, is the second most common reason for failure. Use an appropriate slug control as these pests can demolish a tray of seedlings in the speed of light.

As soon as the seeds sprout, remove the cover, otherwise they will bolt. Germination of spring sowings normally takes from three to seven weeks, but some species can take much longer so don't throw out your seed trays too soon. For instance, *Primula veris* seems to take absolutely ages.

Beware of planting your seeds under glass, as temperatures can rise too high on sunny days even in winter. Ideal germination temperature is between 53°F and 59°F (12–15°C). Lower temperatures do no harm, but anything over 64°F (18°C) is risky.

Primulas establish much faster if a good root system has developed before they are moved, so wait until seedlings have at least four leaves. The seedlings then need to be pricked out into individual pots, larger seed trays, or cell trays. When the young seedlings have well-established roots—the roots are coming out of the end of the pot—they are big enough to be planted out in the ground or into containers.

Seedlings ready to be pricked out.

Cut Flowers

The sale of polyanthus flowers for the cut-flower market used to be a booming industry. In fact, Barnhaven started out in England mainly selling cut flowers. Today, however, primulas as cut flowers are rarely offered for sale, having gone out of fashion in favour of the more exotic blooms available year-round due to rapid air transport. This is a real pity, for primroses make a welcome splash of colour when so little else is available. Not only do they have a huge colour range, but most of them are strongly scented and are an ideal addition to any spring flower arrangement.

On the bright side, there is a recent trend to return to locally grown flowers. A grower in Suffolk, England, told us she used primroses in several ways, as dried flowers for confetti, as pressed flowers, the native primroses as edibles and for drying, and the polyanthus for wedding bouquets and for selling at local markets. Maybe things are changing and it is worth keeping an eye on farmers' markets and for offers on the Internet, but for the time being you will have to grow your own primroses and get creative with beautiful spring bouquets. One small note of warning: certain leaves and stems can cause a skin reaction in some sensitive people.

Any container can be used as a vase—what you use is limited only by your imagination—but since primulas are modest cottagey flowers, they work well in containers that have simple shapes in plain or earthy colours. Small vases of smoked glass or earthenware jars create a lovely old-fashioned effect, as do stemmed goblets, sundae dishes, or

Micro-propagation

THE MODERN METHODS OF tissue-culture and micro-propagation have revolutionized the sale of primulas since the last half of the twentieth century. Most of the primroses in garden centres and many nurseries have been produced this way as it is a cheap, fast, and reliable method of producing uniform plants on a large scale. Without getting too technical, as there are several methods out there, this method of propagation basically consists of breeding plants in test tubes from stem cell materiel. The resulting plants should be exact clones of the original plant.

Today, most commercial primroses are bred for their uniformity, compact growing habit, flowering season, size of flower, and brightness. Some would say this comes at the expense of colour, scent, hardiness, and diversity. However, producers are returning to hardier primroses and scented flowers are now becoming available.

One of the disadvantages of micro-propagation is that the plant material does not always do what it is supposed to do. The genetic material can mutate and produce a "sport." Auriculas are one of the primulas that are difficult to micro-propagate, throwing up some abnormalities. Generally, primulas grow well from seed, which is a way of keeping disease-free and variety-rich plants on the market, and we feel there is no reason to micro-propagate the species unless they are very difficult to obtain from seed.

There are, however, some advantages to tissue culture. For double primroses, which are sterile (they cannot produce seed), the only way to produce enough plants for sale is to divide them manually. Doing this from a single unique plant can take a very long time. In addition, some older hybrids have been kept going by micro-propagation. *Primula* 'Dawn Ansell' is a good example of this. It is possible that without micro-propagation more of these old cultivars would have been lost. So used in combination with traditional methods of seed sowing and manual division, micro-propagation has to be considered a valuable tool for safeguarding some of the old varieties and allowing more people to grow them.

It is also a way of rescuing some varieties that may have become riddled with disease from years of division, which may have weakened the plant. Using the new methods, it is possible to clean up the genetic material and thus safeguard some varieties.

There will always be a demand for certain plants to be painstakingly hand propagated, ensuring a small but select supply and safeguarding the diversity of the gene pool. But there will also be a demand for micro-propagated plants to cater to the mass market. We feel the two methods can exist hand in hand.

Plug plants of Irish Kennedy primroses produced by tissue culture at FitzGerald Nurseries in Ireland.

Primula 'Francisca' displayed in smoked glass bottles.

Double primrose 'Camaieu' in a miniature teapot.

sweet dishes. You can use small baskets by placing a container inside the basket such as a tin can sprayed black.

As a rule, cut the flowers when they are just showing colour, preferably early in the morning. The blooms should last about a week in water if kept in a cool location. To make them last longer, put the flowers in tepid water that comes high up the stem, preferably to just below the flower. Allow the flowers to have a long drink in a cool, draught-free place for a couple of hours before you arrange them.

Sometimes polyanthus droop their heads after being arranged. This problem can usually be solved by pricking the neck of the stem just below the flower head before allowing the stems to soak in water.

The acaulis primroses look prettiest when they are simply bunched in your hand as they are picked, surrounded with some of their own foliage and placed in a small container such as a teacup, cream jug, or wine glass. A few pulmonaria or viola flowers can be added to your bunch. This is the only way to include wild primroses as their stems are rather soft.

The modern hybrids and the double primroses have stronger stems than the wild ones and can be arranged in

Double primrose Belarina Valentine in a simple posy.

an oasis to make a very pretty round or oval mound in a shallow dish. The trick is to achieve a three-dimensional effect by placing the flowers at different heights and lightening the mass by using a variety of flowers and foliage. *Muscari*, forget-me-nots, dwarf daffodils, small-flowered hellebores, and small sprays of catkins from hazel, birch, or alder can all be used, along with small-leaved foliage such as box or cotoneaster. Spiky foliage from rosemary, lavender, santolina, heather, or Lawson cypress can be used to add height. The edges can be softened by using trails of small-leaved ivy or periwinkle.

The polyanthus primrose 'Paris '90', cowslips, daffodils, and scillas make wonderful spring bunches.

The long-stemmed polyanthus flower with its huge colour range makes it an ideal addition to any spring flower arrangement. Jack-in-the-Green forms are among the best flowers for indoor decoration as the green ruff stays fresh for several weeks after the blooms have faded. To make a simple table decoration, place rolled wire netting in a large bowl, then insert the blooms between the wire. The combinations for using polyanthus flowers are infinite but here are some ideas:

- Blue polyanthus with yellow or white miniature daffodils.
- Yellow and crimson polyanthus with sprays of wallflowers.
- Yellow and white polyanthus with vivid purple spikes of *Muscari*.
- Purple polyanthus with white or mauve drumstick primula.

Included in so many bouquets painted in the eighteenth century, auriculas have been completely forgotten as a cut flower. They are stunning flowers though not always easy to combine with other things. Some grey foliage may suffice to give them a lovely backdrop.

One of the best groups of primroses for flower arranging is the hybrids of *Primula sieboldii*. They have long stalks to 12 in. (30 cm) and beautiful, fragile-looking blooms—either lacy or smooth—in a wide range of complementary pastel shades of white, blue, and pink. They are sheer magic by candlelight and can last up to a fortnight in water.

Edible Primroses

All primrose flowers are edible though mainly *Primula veris* and *P. vulgaris* have traditionally been used. The flowers have a very mild, sweet yet slightly peppery taste. Make sure they are picked in a place free from pesticides. It is also possible to eat the leaves, though a word of caution as they may cause an allergic reaction in some people.

Over the years, the whole plant has been used in several different ways. Primulas are said to soothe nerves, ease insomnia, and reduce headaches. Many of the old herbals are a great place to find recipes. For example, a

Primula sieboldii is magical in a vase.

Cupcakes with crystallized primrose flowers.

version of *The Complete Herbal* by Nicholas Culpeper, published in 1653, is still in print and its recipes still in use today.

There are some other lovely ideas and people are returning to the idea of foraging. Many of the recipes require vast quantities of flowers that are not readily available as it is obviously preferable not to pick them in the wild; however, if you have primulas growing in your garden, here are some ideas you might like to try.

- **Primrose salad** Add fresh flowers to decorate your salads and add a splash of colour. Remove the stalks so the flowers sit open-faced on top of lettuce, cress, and other greens.
- **Cowslip wine** Many different recipes are available, all simple and only taking a few weeks to make.

Pancakes with primroses.

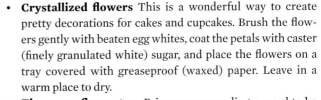

- **Crystallized flowers** This is a wonderful way to create pretty decorations for cakes and cupcakes. Brush the flowers gently with beaten egg whites, coat the petals with caster (finely granulated white) sugar, and place the flowers on a tray covered with greaseproof (waxed) paper. Leave in a warm place to dry.
- **Tisanes or flower teas** Primrose or cowslip tea used to be recommended as a mild sedative for anxiety or insomnia. Put two teaspoons of the fresh or dried flowers in a jug and cover with boiling water. Allow to infuse for five minutes and then strain into a cup. Sweeten with sugar or honey to taste.
- **Primrose pancake** When making pancakes, cook them on one side well, then place the primroses on the top "wet side" before flipping; cook for a shorter time than the original side to ensure the flowers maintain their colour.

WHERE TO BUY

International Shipping

IMPORTING TO THE UNITED STATES FROM EUROPE

Both seeds and plants can be imported to the United States from Europe. A phyto-sanitary certificate is needed. You can get a free Small Lots permit for seed from the Animal and Plant Health Inspection Service. Some European growers will provide all the necessary certification for a fee. Plants have to be sent bare-rooted.

IMPORTING TO CANADA FROM EUROPE

An import and phyto-sanitary certificate is necessary for bare-rooted plants but not for seed.

IMPORTING TO EUROPE FROM COUNTRIES OUTSIDE THE EUROPEAN UNION

A phyto-sanitary certificate is required for plants from the country sending out the plants. No certificate is needed to import small quantities of primula seed.

IMPORTING WITHIN THE EUROPEAN UNION

No certificates are needed for primula plants or seed shipped within the European Union.

CANADA

Fraser's Thimble Farm
175 Arbutus Road
Salt Spring Island,
British Columbia V8K 1A3
www.thimblefarms.com
A selection of Primula *species. Mail order available to the United States.*

Lost Horizons
5654 Highway #7
Acton, Ontario L7J 2L7
www.losthorizons.ca
A wide choice of Asiatic, double, and alpine primulas for local pick-up only.

Wrightman Alpines Nursery
480 Brandy Cove Road
Saint Andrews, New Brunswick E5B 2P9
www.wrightmanalpines.com
Choice alpine and rock garden plants. Many primulas by mail order, including auriculas. Display gardens.

FRANCE

Barnhaven Primroses
Keranguiner
22310, Plestin-les-grèves
www.barnhaven.com
Large choice of seed and plants. Holder of a National Plant Collection for Barnhaven strains and auricula cultivars. Will ship to most countries worldwide with the necessary certification. Website in French, English, and German.

Jelitto Perennial Seeds

29685 Schwarmstedt
Postfach 1264
www.jelitto.com
A wide selection of Primula *seeds. Mail order worldwide. Website in German and English.*

Staudengärtnerei Peters

Allerlei Seltenes
Auf dem Flidd 20
25436 Uetersen
www.alpine-peters.de
Large selection of alpines, auriculas, and some sieboldii hybrids. Will ship to countries outside of Europe with certification.

Abriachan Garden Nursery

Kilianan
Loch Ness-Side
Inverness
Scotland IV3 8LA
www.lochnessgarden.com
Wonderful woodland gardens on the shores of Loch Ness that are well worth a visit. An extensive collection of old, named double and single primroses, auriculas, and species. Mail-order service within the United Kingdom.

Angusplants

3 Balfour Cottages
Menmuir
By Brechin
Angus
Scotland DD9 7RN
www.angusplants.co.uk
A small family-run nursery specializing in Primula auricula. *Holder of a National Plant Collection of Alpine auriculas. Mail-order service available in the United Kingdom and Europe.*

Ardfearn Nursery

Bunchrew
Inverness
Scotland IV3 8RH
www.ardfearn-nursery.co.uk
Good selection of primulas. Mail-order delivery in the United Kingdom and Europe.

Ashwoods Nurseries

Ashwood Lower Lane
Kingswinford
West Midlands
England DY6 0AE
www.ashwoodnurseries.com
A large garden centre with a collection of Primula auricula. *Nursery owner John Massey's private gardens, which are next to the garden centre, are a delight to visit in spring. Look out for the open days. Mail-order service available in the United Kingdom and Europe.*

Chiltern Seeds

Crowmarsh Battle Barns
114 Preston Crowmarsh
Wallingford
England OX10 6SL
www.chilternseeds.co.uk
A wide range of Primula *seed.*

Crescent Plants

Stoney Cross
Marden
Hereford
England HR1 3EW
www.auriculas.co.uk
Auricula specialist. Visitors by appointment. Mail-order service in the United Kingdom.

Drointon Nurseries
Plaster Pitts
Ripon
North Yorkshire
England HG4 5EF
www.auricula-plants.co.uk
Primula auricula *specialists. Holder of
a National Collection of border auriculas. Opening times by appointment or open
days in spring. Mail-order service. Will ship
overseas.*

Edrom Nurseries and Gardens
School Road
Coldingham
Eyemouth
Berwickshire
Scotland TD14 5TZ
www.edrom-nurseries.co.uk
*A wide choice of old varieties and rare
plants, Asiatic primulas, and alpines.*

Farmyard Nurseries
Dol Llan Road
Llandysul
Carmarthenshire
Wales SA44 4RL
www.farmyardnurseries.co.uk
A selection of Primula auricula *and* P. sie-
boldii *cultivars. Mail order to the United
Kingdom and Europe.*

Field House Nursery
Leake Road
Gotham
Nottingham
England NG11 0JN
*Specialist collections of auricula, alpine
primula, and other primrose and polyan-
thus. Holder of a National Plant Collec-
tion of Alpine and Show auriculas. A link to
their PDF catalogue is found on the NAPS
Midland and West website (www.auricula
andprimula.org.uk); scroll down for link.
Seed (but not plants) also available by
mail order.*

ForageFor
Suffolk
England
www.foragefor.co.uk
*A small cut-flower company that grows its
own flowers and often includes primroses in
its bouquets. Markets, weddings, and flower
delivery.*

Hillview Hardy Plants
Worfield
Near Bridgnorth
Shropshire
England WV15 5NT
www.hillviewhardyplants.com/
*Auriculas, primulas, and other hardy
perennials.*

Kevock Garden Plants
16 Kevock Road
Lasswade
Midlothian
Scotland EH18 1HT
www.kevockgarden.co.uk
*A nursery specializing in unusual alpine,
woodland, and bog plants. A huge choice of
primulas available by mail order, including
some rarer species. A valley garden available to visit by appointment only. Guided
tours available for groups.*

Larch Cottage Nurseries
Melkinthorpe
Penrith
Cumbria
England CA10 2DR
www.larchcottage.co.uk
*Select choice of primroses and Asiatic prim-
ulas. Mail-order service to the United King-
dom and Europe.*

Messers W. and S. Lockyer
39 Mitchley Avenue
Riddlesdown
Purley
Surrey
England CR8 1BZ
+44(0)20 8660 1336
Auricula specialists but also primroses, polyanthus, and spring bulbs. Holder of a National Collection of double auriculas.

Monksilver Nursery
Oakington Road
Cottenham
Cambridge
England CB24 8TW
www.monksilvernursery.co.uk
Small collection of old, named primrose cultivars. Mail-order service available in the United Kingdom and Europe.

Owl's Acre Seeds
Yew Tree Cottage
Foston on the Wolds
Driffield
E. Yorks
England YO25 8BJ
www.sweetpea-seed.com
Seed of select strains of Primula *from specialist breeders.*

Peninsula Primulas
72 Balleasborough Road
Kircubbin, County Down
Northern Ireland BT22 1AD
www.penprimulas.com
Large selection of primulas. Plants sent bare-rooted to the United Kingdom and Ireland.

Plant World Seeds
St Marychurch Road
Newton Abbot
Devon
England TQ12 4SE
www.plant-world-seeds.com

Pop's Plants
Pop's Cottage
Barford Lane
Downton
Salisbury
Wiltshire
England SP5 3PZ
www.popsplants.co.uk
A small private nursery specializing in named cultivars of Primula auricula, *all produced from plants in the nursery's four National Plant Collections (show, alpine, double, striped) of some 1200 named cultivars. Only open to visitors by appointment. Mail-order service to overseas.*

Ryal Nursery
East Farm Cottage
Ryal
Northumberland
England NE20 0SA
+44(0)1661 886562
Holder of a National Collection of Primula marginata *and hybrids. Visits by appointment. No mail-order service.*

Staddon Farm Nurseries
North Devon
England
www.pennysprimulas.co.uk
Holder of a National Plant Collection of Primula sieboldii *Japanese cultivars. Mail-order service in the United Kingdom and Europe. Visits by appointment only.*

Summerdale Garden and Nursery
Summerdale House
Cow Brow
Lupton
Carnforth
Cumbria
England LA6 1PE
www.summerdalegardenplants.co.uk
Very large collection of primulas including Barnhaven hybrids. The garden is open on special open days. Mail-order service for some plants to the United Kingdom.

Woottens of Wenhaston
Blackheath
Wenhaston
Halesworth
Suffolk
England 1P19 9HD
www.woottensplants.com
Large collection of auriculas. Mail-order delivery to the United Kingdom and Europe.

UNITED STATES

Annie's Annuals and Perennials
740 Market Avenue
Richmond, California 94801
www.anniesannuals.com
A few auriculas and gold-laced for sale.

Arrowhead Alpines
1310 North Gregory Road
P.O. Box 857
Fowlerville, Michigan 48836
www.arrowheadalpines.com
Retail and mail-order plant nursery with a large choice of alpine primulas and other species.

Cady's Falls Nursery
Don and Lela Avery
637 Duahmel Road
Morrisville, Vermont 05661
www.cadysfallsnursery.com
A lovely garden to visit and a wide choice of primulas including some P. kisoana, P. denticulata, *and a large choice of double primroses. Local pick-up only.*

Carolyn's Shade Gardens
325 South Roberts Road
Bryn Mawr, Pennsylvania 19010
www.carolynsshadegardens.com
Retail nursery, no mail order for primulas. Garden well worth the visit. Small collection of primulas including sieboldii and candelabras.

Edelweiss Perennials
29800 South Barlow Road
Canby, Oregon 97013
www.edelweissperennials.com
Small collection of auriculas and primula. Mail-order nursery.

Far Reaches Farm
1818 Hastings Avenue
Port Townsend, Washington 98368
www.farreachesfarm.com
Some unusual species and old cultivars. Mail-order service for most states including Alaska and Hawaii.

Forest Farm
14643 Watergap Road
Williams, Oregon 97544
www.forestfarm.com
Small selection of double primroses.

Joe Pye Weed's Garden
337 Acton Street
Carslisle, Massachusetts 01741
www.jpwflowers.com
A few primroses and P. sieboldii *cultivars.*

Joy Creek Nursery
20300 NW Watson Road
Scappoose, Oregon 97056
www.joycreek.com
*Retail and mail-order nursery with a small
collection of cowichan, gold-laced, and a
few other named primroses.*

Lazy S'S Farm Nursery
2360 Spotswood Trail
Barboursville, Virginia 22923
www.lazyssfarm.com
*A retail mail-order nursery with a selection
of* Primula sieboldii *available.*

Mountain Brook Primroses
373 Elbow Pond Road
Andover, New Hampshire 03216
www.mtnbrook.com
A small nursery growing some Primula
*hybrids such as gold-laced, cowichans, and
auriculas. Offers a mail-order service.*

Perennial Pleasures Nursery
63 Brickhouse Road
East Hardwick, Vermont 05836
www.perennialpleasures.net
*A small selection of old varieties. Mail
order in the United States and Canada. Display gardens.*

Primrose Hill Woodlanders
421 Birch Road
Brandon, Vermont 05733
www.primrosehillwoodlanders.com
An ever-expanding selection of Primula
*species and hybrids sold at specialty plant
sales around the Northeast and by appointment at the nursery.*

Sequim Rare Plants
500 North Sequim Avenue
Sequim, Washington 98382
www.sequimrareplants.com
A selection of Primula auricula *and a
few other* Primula *hybrids. Mail order
available.*

Sunshine Farm and Gardens
696 Glicks Road
Renick, West Virginia 24966
www.sunfarm.com
A small selection of Primula japonica, P.
sieboldii, *and a few primrose cultivars.
Mail order available.*

Wild Ginger Farm
24000 South Schuebel School Road
Beavercreek, Oregon 97004
www.wildgingerfarm.com
*Plants for sale on-site and at regional plants
sales. Small selection of primulas including alpine and some of their own P. sieboldii hybrids.*

WHERE TO SEE

What better way to get inspiration for your own garden than to visit some of the wonderful public and private gardens who use primroses to show them off to their best advantage. Sometimes a walk in your local park and a look at the town plantings combining other spring annuals can be enough to give you ideas but if you are looking for something really special, there are plenty of gardens that have huge collections of primulas waiting to be discovered.

Although the United Kingdom is reputed for its love of all things primrose there are many other beautiful gardens in the Northern Hemisphere including Alaska and Sweden! We have included here some of the un-missable gardens with extended collections, however there are many smaller gardens with wonderful displays that you may come across on open garden schemes, though to list them all would be impossible. For more information the Auricula and Primula Societies are always a good place to start.

CANADA

Butchart Gardens
800 Benvenuto Avenue
Brentwood Bay
British Columbia V8M 1J8
www.butchartgardens.com

Darts Hill Garden Park
16th Avenue (at 170th Street)
Surrey, British Columbia V3S 9X3
www.dartshill.ca

Devonian Botanic Garden
51227 AB-60
Parkland County
Alberta T7Y 1C5
www.devonian.ualberta.ca

University of British Columbia Botanical Garden
6804 WS Marine Drive
Vancouver, British Columbia V6T 1Z4
www.botanicalgarden.ubc.ca

IRELAND

Blarney Castle and Gardens
Blarney
Cork
www.blarneycastle.ie
Mass plantings of Kennedy primroses. They are developing a collection of Irish Heritage plants, a good project to keep an eye on. Best time to visit is early spring.

Caher Bridge Garden
Carl Wright
Formoyle West
Fanore
County Clare
www.discoverireland.ie/Arts-Culture-Heritage/caher-bridge-garden/76427
A private garden, a real plantsman's delight with a large collection of Primula. *Guided tours by appointment from March to October.*

June Blake's Garden
Tinode
Blessington
County Wicklow
www.juneblake.ie
Open from April to September. Watch out for the special June Blake primrose.

Tromsø Arctic-Alpine Botanic Garden
Tromsø
9006 Tromsø
www.en.uit.no/om/enhet/tmu/botanisk
The world's northernmost botanical garden is something rather special and says something about primulas coping in extreme locations. Wonderful collection of alpine primulas.

SWEDEN

Gothenburg Botanical Garden
Carl Skottsbergs Gata 22 A
413 19 Göteborg
www.goteborg.com/en/botaniska-tradgarden
A large collection of Primula *in this well-reputed botanical garden.*

UNITED KINGDOM

Bodnant Garden
Tal-y-Cafn
Colwyn Bay
Conwy
Wales LL28 5RE
www.bodnantgarden.co.uk
Boasts an extensive collection of Primula. *Just planted a new Primula Path.*

Bowood House and Gardens
Calne
Wiltshire
England SN11 0LZ
www.bowood.org/bowood-gardens
For six weeks from mid-April until early June, the rhododendron woodland garden puts on a fine display. Plenty of candelabra primulas planted down by the streams meandering through the woodland.

Calke Abbey
Ticknall
Derby
Derbyshire
England DE73 7LE
www.nationaltrust.org.uk/calke-abbey
The largest auricula theatre around, built in 1830, it is thought to be one of the oldest of its kind. Best time to see it is April or May; check for the flowering period before your visit to avoid disappointment.

Cluny House Gardens
Cluny House
Aberfeldy
Perthshire
Scotland PH15 2JT
www.clunyhousegardens.com
A lovely woodland garden. Many plants from the Himalayas including an extensive collection of Asiatic primulas.

Explorers Garden
Port-Na-Craig
Pitlochry
Perthshire
Scotland PH16 5DR
www.explorersgarden.com
A newer garden which aims to present a collection of plants introduced by Scottish explorers including some primulas.

Fairhaven Woodland and Water Garden
The Fairhaven Garden Trust
School Road
South Walsham
Norfolk
England NR13 6DZ
www.fairhavengarden.co.uk
A collection of naturalized candelabra primulas. The best time to visit is the last two weeks of May and first two weeks of June.

Glebe Garden
The Glebe
North Petherwin
Launceston
Cornwall
England PL15 8LR
www.glebegarden.co.uk
Holder of a National Collection of double primroses (Primula vulgaris and hybrids). Visits of the collection by appointment. Garden open to groups by appointment only.

Glendoick Gardens
Glendoick
Glencarse
Perth
Scotland PH2 7NS
www.glendoick.com
A great place to see many Asiatic primulas. Open in April and May.

Marwood Hill Garden
Marwood
Barnstaple
North Devon
England EX31 4EB
www.marwoodhillgarden.co.uk
Worth a visit for the bog gardens where the candelabra primulas and irises put on a lovely display.

Ragley House and Gardens
Ragley
Alcester
Warwickshire
England B49 5NJ
www.ragley.co.uk
A lovely winter garden to visit. Also has a crevice garden for alpine plants.

Regina's Cottage
Pat and Robin Fisher
Blaencwm Cottage
Foelgastell
Llanelli
Wales SA14 7HL
www.reginascottage.com
Holders of a National Collection of border auriculas displayed in pots in open-sided pavilion, flower shed, and cold frames. Also in raised beds in garden. Open days in May or by appointment.

RHS Garden Harlow Carr
Crag Lane
Harrogate
North Yorkshire
England HG3 1QB
www.rhs.org.uk/gardens/harlow-carr
Large collection of primulas and an alpine house. Especially stunning is the streamside planting of candelabra primulas.

RHS Garden Kew
Royal Botanic Gardens
Kew
Richmond
Surrey
England TW9 3AB
www.kew.org
A large collection of primulas and alpine house.

RHS Garden Rosemoor
Great Torrington
Devon
England EX38 8PH
www.rhs.org.uk/gardens/rosemoor
Home to an extended collection of Primula*, especially Asiatic species. It has just inherited the* P. sieboldii *collection from Kew, so look for them in the garden and on display in the alpine house. Plenty of other primulas in the winter garden.*

RHS Garden Wisley
Woking
Surrey
England GU23 6QB
www.rhs.org.uk/gardens/wisley
Extensive collection of Asiatic species including some gems in the alpine house, rockery, and in a stunning crevice garden.

Rowallane Garden
Saintfield
County Down
Northern Ireland BT24 7LH
www.nationaltrust.org.uk/rowallane-garden
Best time to visit in April and May. Stunning natural rock garden with a display of Mecanopsis *and* Primula*. Look for* Primula *'Rowallene Rose'.*

Royal Botanic Garden Edinburgh
Inverleith Row
Arboretum Place
Edinburgh
Scotland EH3 5LR
www.rbge.org.uk
One of the most extensive collections of primulas in the world! Definitely worth a visit.

Temple Newsam Estate
Temple Newsam Rd
Off Selby Rd
Leeds
England LS15 0AE
A 1500-acre park once landscaped by Capability Brown. Holder of a National Plant Collection of Alpine auriculas.

Timpany Nurseries and Gardens
77, Magheratimpany Road
Ballynahinch
County Down
Northern Ireland BT24 8PA
www.timpanynurseries.com

Trebah Garden
Trebah Garden Trust
Mawnan Smith
Near Falmouth
Cornwall
England TR11 5JZ
www.trebahgarden.co.uk
Known for its wonderful displays of candelabra primulas.

Dr M. Webster
18 Lye Mead
Winford
Bristol
England BS40 8AU
+44(0)1275 472818
National Collection Holder of Primula
*(British Floral Variants). Specializing in
many of the anomalous primroses. There
is a small garden and 2 cold greenhouses to
visit. By appointment only.*

UNITED STATES

Bellevue Botanical Garden
12001 Main Street
Bellevue, Washington 98005
www.bellevuebotanical.org

Chanticleer
786 Church Road
Wayne, Pennsylvania 19087
www.chanticleergarden.org
*An amazing garden. The Asian woods are
awash with* P. sieboldii *and other species.*

Coastal Maine Botanical Gardens
132 Botanical Gardens Drive
Boothbay, Maine 04537
www.mainegardens.org

Denver Botanic Gardens
1007 York Street
Denver, Colorado 80206
www.botanicgardens.org
*An impressive collection of primulas espe-
cially present in the alpine collection for
which they have collection status from
North American Plant Collections Consortium (NAPCC).*

**Elisabeth Carey Miller Botanical
Garden**
P.O. Box 77377
Seatlle, Washington 98177
www.millergarden.org

Jensen-Olson Arboretum
23035 Glacier Highway
Juneau, Alaska 99801
www.juneau.org/parkrec/arboretum-
main.php
*An incredible location for this public garden
on the east shore of Favorite Channel. Has
collection status for Primula from North
American Plant Collections Consortium
(NAPCC).*

Juniper Level Botanic Garden
9241 Sauls Road
Raleigh, North Carolina 27603
www.jlbg.org
Also a nursery onsite. Large collection of
Primula sieboldii *cultivars.*

New York Botanical Garden
2900 Southern Boulevard
Bronx, New York 10458
www.nybg.org

Tower Hill Botanic Garden
11 French Drive
Boylston, Massachusetts 01505
www.towerhillbg.org

Winterthur Quarry Garden
5105 Kennet Pike
Wilmington, Delaware 19735
www.winterthur.org

FOR MORE INFORMATION

BOOKS

Baker, Gwen, and Peter Ward. 1995. *Auriculas*. London: Batsford.

Cleveland-Peck, Patricia. 2011. *Auriculas Through the Ages: Bear's Ears, Ricklers and Painted Ladies*. Ramsbury, England: Crowood Press.

Corsar, Kenneth Charles. 1952. *Primulas in the Garden*. London: G. Bles.

Dorey, Paul. 2011. *Auriculas: An Essential Guide*. Malborough, England: Crowood Press.

Duthie, Ruth. 1988. *Florists' Flowers and Societies*. Aylesbury, England: Shire Garden History.

Genders, Roy. 1963. *The Polyanthus: Its History and Culture*. Newton, Massachusetts: C. T. Branford.

Genders, Roy. 1958. *Auriculas*. London: John Gifford.

Green, Roy. 1976. *Asiatic Primulas: A Gardener's Guide*. Woking, England: Alpine Garden Society.

Guest, Allan. 2009. The *Auricula: History, Cultivation and Varieties*. New York: Garden Art Press.

Halda, Josef J. 1992. *The Genus Primula in Cultivation and the Wild*. Denver, Colorado: Tethys Books.

Hecker, W. R. 1971. *Auriculas and Primroses*. London: Batsford.

Hyatt, Brenda. 1996. *Auriculas: Their Care and Cultivation*. London: Cassell.

Hyatt, Brenda. 1989. *Primroses and Auriculas*. 2nd edition. London: Cassell.

Lyall, H. G. *Hardy Primulas*. London: W. H. & L. Collingridge.

Puttock, A. G. *Primulas*. London: John Gifford.

Richards, John. 2003. *Primula*. New edition. Portland, Oregon: Timber Press.

Robinson, Mary A. 2000. *Auriculas for Everyone: How to Grow and Show Perfect Plants*. Lewes, England: Guild of Master Craftsman Publications.

Robinson, Mary A. 1990. *Primulas: The Complete Guide*. Swindon, England: Crowood Press.

Smith G. F., B. Burrow, and D. B. Lowe. 1984. *Primulas of Europe and America*. Woking, England: Alpine Garden Society.

Shaw, Barbara. 1991. *The Book of Prim-roses*. Portland, Oregon: Timber Press.

Swindells, Philip. 1989. *A Plantsman's Guide to Primulas*. London: Ward Lock.

Ward, Peter. 1997. *Primroses and Polyanthus*. London: Batsford.

Ward, Peter. 2008. *Primroses and Auriculas*. RHS Wisley Handbooks. London: Mitchell Beazley.

Wemyss-Cooke, Jack. 1986. *Primulas Old and New: Auriculas, Primulas, Primroses, Polyanthus*. LondonL: David and Charles.

WEBSITES

Primula World: www.primulaworld.com. A visual reference for the genus *Primula* compiled by Pam Eveleigh. This is a fantastic resource for any primula grower. It has detailed descriptions and photos of nearly all the primula species, including many taken in the wild.

ORGANIZATIONS

These wonderful institutions are a stalwart for the promotion of plants all over the world.. Very much part of British gardening life during the eighteenth century, it is very likely that the first Primula and Auricula Societies were inspired by some of the existing societies on the continent and that the Flemish Huguenot immigrants brought the tradition with them. Whereas they may have started as the prerogative of wealthy or aristocratic florists by the mid-eighteenth century, saddlers, weavers and barbers are listed among the growers and the feasts were often held in the local inn. The prizes were quite substantial and included china bowls, silver spoons and the iconic copper kettle. Only *Primula auricula* and the *P.* Gold-laced Group were considered to be worthy as florist flowers and the first societies were dedicated to these plants. However, now there is more interest in the genus as a whole, and open classes at the shows.

They have regular shows in the spring, and participate in plant fairs and national shows, publish regular journals and swop seeds and plants. It is not just an excuse for having a party with like minded people (though pubs and feasts have always come into it), over the years there have been some extremely important amateur growers who have contributed much to introducing new and better hybrids to our gardens. There have been botanists and researchers who regularly publish articles in the journals, plant hunters who have found new undiscovered gems and the growers who have kept some of the little known and rarer species alive which would have been overlooked by the plant growing industry. They are also very supportive of new growers and gladly share cultural information with beginners. These last few years have seen dwindling membership in some of the groups but with the advent of new social media, forums, facebook pages, journals and blogs have started to proliferate and some of the seed exchanges are now some of the largest in the world, reuniting people who would never have had the opportunity to communicate before.

Alpine Garden Society (AGS): www.alpinegardensociety.net. Based in England, the AGS aims to bring together anyone interested in alpine or rock garden plants in general, though primulas often feature in many of the articles on its website and in its journal. There is a particular emphasis on botanical species and understandably on *Primula allionii* and *P. marginata* hybrids. The AGS also includes special *Primula* classes in its regular shows in England, Ireland, and Wales. The AGS has local groups in the United Kingdom and Ireland and runs a seed exchange. Of particular interest on the AGS website are the Garden Diaries with some great tips and inspiring photos by expert gardeners.

American Primrose Society: www.americanprimrosesociety.org. This society was founded in 1941 and aims to bring *Primula* enthusiasts together. There are several chapters that hold regular meetings (Juneau, Tacoma, New England, and British Columbia). They are very welcoming to new members and are a great source of information on growing primulas. They also run a seed exchange with donors from all over the world. They produce a quarterly magazine and have many links with growers in Europe.

Irish Garden Plant Society: www.irishgardenplantsociety.com.

National Auricula and Primula Society: www.auriculaandprimula.org.uk (Midlands and West Section), www.auriculas.org.uk (Northern Section), www.southernauriculaprimula.org.uk (Southern Section). The society has several local groups all over the United Kingdom, most of which are long-running societies established at the end of the nineteenth century. They have a particular interest in auriculas and gold-laced primulas, although you will find many of the European primulas at the shows. They publish a year book, hold an annual meeting, and hold three shows a year where plant sales usually take place.

North American Rock Garden Society (NARGS): www.nargs.org. A very active society aimed at promoting alpine plants with several chapters all over the United States. They hold talks with specialist speakers and organize tours, plant sales, a seed exchange and animate a forum. Primulas often feature in their literature.

Scottish Auricula and Primula Society: www.thescottishauriculaandprimulasociety.co.uk. This society is still in its infancy in a bid to revive the old Scottish Primula and Auricula Society which was founded in 1887. With the backing of some prominent growers and plant breeders, the first show was held in May 2015. The objectives of the society are to stimulate interest, exhibit, improve, conserve and further the cultivation of auriculas and primulas.

Scottish Rock Garden club: www.srgc.net/. The Scottish Rock Garden club was founded in 1933 by a small group of enthusiasts who were interested in promoting the cultivation of alpine and rock garden plants through meetings and shows. Over the years they have added a journal, a conference, a website and a forum. It has a very international membership and one of the best seed exchanges. The forum is an extremely lively and friendly place with many experts but also amateur growers who post many pictures of plants and share information. There is a whole section dedicated to primulas.

HARDINESS ZONE TEMPERATURES

Temp °F			Zone	Temp °C		
-60	to	-55	1a	-51	to	-48
-55	to	-50	1b	-48	to	-46
-50	to	-45	2a	-46	to	-43
-45	to	-40	2b	-43	to	-40
-40	to	-35	3a	-40	to	-37
-35	to	-30	3b	-37	to	-34
-30	to	-25	4a	-34	to	-32
-25	to	-20	4b	-32	to	-29
-20	to	-15	5a	-29	to	-26
-15	to	-10	5b	-26	to	-23
-10	to	-5	6a	-23	to	-21
-5	to	0	6b	-21	to	-18
0	to	5	7a	-18	to	-15
5	to	10	7b	-15	to	-12
10	to	15	8a	-12	to	-9
15	to	20	8b	-9	to	-7
20	to	25	9a	-7	to	-4
25	to	30	9b	-4	to	-1
30	to	35	10a	-1	to	2
35	to	40	10b	2	to	4
40	to	45	11a	4	to	7
45	to	50	11b	7	to	10
50	to	55	12a	10	to	13
55	to	60	12b	13	to	16
60	to	65	13a	16	to	18
65	to	70	13b	18	to	21

FIND HARDINESS MAPS ON THE INTERNET

United States usna.usda.gov/Hardzone/ushzmap.html
Canada planthardiness.gc.ca
Europe houzz.com/europeZoneFinder

ACKNOWLEDGEMENTS

Writing a book while running a busy nursery has proved to be a challenge, albeit a very rewarding one. It would have been impossible to undertake without the help and support of our friends and family. So first and foremost a big thanks to Rob Mitchell and David Lawson for the moral support, encouragement, proofreading, and cups of tea, and Daniel Lawson for his expert photography.

We would like to give a big thank you to the many, many people who have helped with the choice of plants and photos and given advice. It has definitely proved that primula growers are, like the plants that they grow, a charming and delightfully helpful bunch. We would especially like to thank the various nurseries and primula specialists such as Val Woolley from Fieldhouse alpines, David Rankin from Kevock Gardens, Melvyn and Penny Jones from Staddon Farm Nurseries, Pam Eveleigh who runs the Primula World website, Alison and Mark Hutson from Angus Plants, Pat Fitzgerald, Caroline Stone, and Pat and Robin Fisher.

We have also had help from many botanical gardens and private gardens, which have been forthcoming with information about their collections. Special thanks go to Merrill Jensen from the Jensen-Olson Arboretum and to Richard Wilson from Kew Gardens.

Many plant society members have been very generous with their time. A special mention goes to Amy Olmsted from the American Primrose Society, John Richards from the Alpine Garden Society, Terry Mitchell and the National Auricula and Primula Societies in the United Kingdom, members of the National Alpine and Rock Garden Society, Sophie Le Berre from the CCVS (French Society for the Preservation of Plant Collections), Mr Torii from the Japanese Sakurasō Society, and members of the Scottish Rock Garden Society. Thanks as well to Angela Bradford for the proofreading of some chapters and her flower-arranging skills.

We would also like to thank the team at Timber Press, Anna Mumford and Linda Willms, for their patience and hard work throughout the whole process.

Last of all but certainly not least, a very big heartfelt thank you goes to all the Barnhaven customers, many who helped with photos, for all their encouragement and support over the years.

PHOTO CREDITS

All photos by Barnhaven Primroses (Daniel Lawson, Lynne Lawson, and Jodie Mitchell), except as noted below:

TONY AVENT, JUNIPER LEVEL BOTANIC GARDEN AND PLANT DELIGHTS NURSERY, pages 138, 142 right.

HILARY H. BIRKS, pages 51, 100, 130, 155.

SYLVIE COTELLE, pages 136–137, 172, 177.

SIMON CRAWFORD, page 104.

ANNE-MARIE CURTIN, FORAGEFOR, pages 217 top and bottom right, 218 top, 219 bottom.

CLAUDINE DENIAU, pages 18–19 top.

PAM EVELEIGH, PRIMULA WORLD, pages 23 top, 154.

PAT FISHER, page 39 top left (location: Regina's Cottage).

PAT FITZGERALD, FITZGERALD NURSERIES, page 216.

SALLY FORWOOD, page 20 top and bottom

GAP / ANNIE GREEN-ARMYTAGE, pages 26 top, 110 bottom right.

GAP / MARCUS HARPER, page 12 (design: Jill Foxley).

GAP / MICHAEL HOWES, page 165 (location: RHS Spring Flower Show).

GAP / JOANNA KOSSAK, page 70.

GAP / GERALD MAJUMDAR, page 28 (design: David and Olive Mason).

GAP / TREVOR NICHOLSON CHRISTIE, page 18 bottom.

GAP / J. S. SIRA, page 122 (East Village Garden, design: Michael Balston and Marie-Louise Agius, sponsor: Delancey).

GAP/ JAN SMITH, front cover, page 118.

GAP / JULIETTE WADE, page 96 bottom left.

JOHN GLOVER, page 13 (design: Jackie Giles).

MALCOLM GOLDTHORP, page 195 (location: Furzey Gardens).

ANTHONY HISGETT, page 64.

NEIL HULME, page 41.

MARK HUTSON, ANGUS PLANTS, page 58 top.

ROB AND SHARON ILLINGWORTH, pages 26 bottom, 31, 98, 103, 151, 196, 197.

JASON INGRAM, JASON INGRAM PHOTOGRAPHY, pages 66, 67 right and left, 72 top, 81 top and bottom, 86, 94 top, 102, 109.

MIKE IRELAND, pages 156, 158–159 (location: Mike Ireland's Alpine Garden), 163.

TAKUYA IZUMI, SHIKOKU GARDEN, page 135.

MERRILL JENSEN, pages 2–3, 4, 14–15 top, 128, 149, 133, 149, 150, 157, 191 (location: Jensen Olson Arboretum).

MELVYN JONES, STADDON FARM NURSERIES, pages 142 left, 144.

NEIL KENMUIR, page 90.

ANNE-MARIE LEROY, page 35 bottom (location: Japan).

ANDREW LESLIE, GARDENING AT THE EDGE BLOG, pages 113, 119.

SIRPA MIKKOLA, page 101.

TERRY MITCHELL, pages 52, 182.

VINCENT MOINARD, page 185.

NATIONAL TRUST IMAGES / ROGER COULAM, page 23 bottom.

OLIVIER PICHARD, page 50 top.

STEPHEN PLANT, pages 5, 21.

WOLFGANG POMPER, page 44.

DAVID RANKIN, pages 30, 32, 49 (location: Kevock Garden, Scotland).

GILLES REGUER, pages 7 bottom, 246.

HOWARD RICE, pages 34, 38 top right, 83, 84.

JOHN RICHARDS, pages 14, 15 right, 33, 51.

LOUISE ROUT, page 22 (location: Fairhaven Woodland and Water garden).

MARK SCHOFIELD, pages 6–7 top, 40 bottom.

CAROLINE STONE, NATIONAL COLLECTION OF DOUBLE PRIMROSES, page 93.

PADDY TOBIN, pages 97, 99.

TSUNEO TORII, JAPANESE SAKURASŌ SOCIETY, page 54.

SUE TURNER, FROM SEWING ROOM TO POTTING SHED BLOG, pages 38 bottom, 53.

ANNIE VALLADEAU, pages 150, 180.

DYLAN VAUGHAN, FITZGERALD NURSERIES, pages 10–11, 19 bottom, 39 top right, 46, 72 bottom, 78, 192.

RICHARD WILFORD, pages 115, 131, 199 (location: Kew Gardens).

ROBERT WILKINSON, pages 50 top, 173.

JULIE WITMER, GARDENER BLOG, pages 29, 198, 208–209.

CARL WRIGHT, pages 16, 111 (location: Caher Bridge Garden).

IAN YOUNG, page 24.

INDEX

ABOUT THE AUTHORS

LYNNE LAWSON and her daughter, **JODIE MITCHELL**, are specialist growers of primroses. Along with their husbands, David and Rob, they operate world-famous Barnhaven Primroses, now located in northwestern France. Holder of a National Plant Collection for Barnhaven strains and a certified collection of *Primula auricula* cultivars, the nursery continues the 80-year-old tradition of hand pollination begun by Florence Bellis in the United States and carefully maintains the breeding lines Bellis developed. Breeding new varieties of hardy primroses and maintaining rare species and cultivars in cultivation are a vital part of work in the nursery.

Front cover: A candelabra primrose.
Spine: *Primula* Indian Reds Group (top), *P.* Cowichan Blue Group (bottom).
Title page: Primulas at Jensen-Olson Arboretum in Alaska.
Contents page: *Primula vialii* (left), *Primula sieboldii* Manakoora Group
(right).

The Haseltine Building
133 S.W. Second Avenue, Suite 450
Portland, Oregon 97204-3527
timberpress.com

Library of Congress Cataloging-in-Publication Data

Names: Mitchell, Jodie, author | Lawson, Lynne, author.
Title: The plant lover's guide to primulas / Jodie Mitchell & Lynne Lawson.
Description: Portland, Oregon : Timber Press, 2016. | Includes index.
Identifiers: LCCN 2015036651 | ISBN 9781604696455
Subjects: LCSH: Primroses.
Classification: LCC SB413.P7 M58 2016 | DDC 635.9/33675—dc23 LC
    record available at http://lccn.loc.gov/2015036651

A catalog record for this book is also available from the British Library.

Series design by Laken Wright
Cover design by Kristi Pfeffer
Printed in China

THE PLANT LOVER'S GUIDE TO
DAHLIAS
ANDY VERNON

THE PLANT LOVER'S GUIDE TO
SEDUMS
BRENT HORVATH

THE PLANT LOVER'S GUIDE TO
SNOWDROPS
NAOMI SLADE

THE PLANT LOVER'S GUIDE TO
SALVIAS
JOHN WHITTLESEY

THE PLANT LOVER'S GUIDE TO
TULIPS
RICHARD WILFORD

THE PLANT LOVER'S GUIDE TO
FERNS
RICHIE STEFFEN & SUE OLSEN

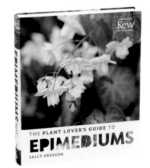

THE PLANT LOVER'S GUIDE TO
EPIMEDIUMS
SALLY GREGSON

THE PLANT LOVER'S GUIDE TO
ASTERS
PAUL PICTON & HELEN PICTON

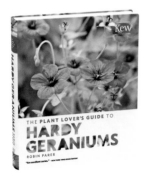

THE PLANT LOVER'S GUIDE TO
HARDY GERANIUMS
ROBIN PARER

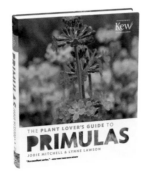

THE PLANT LOVER'S GUIDE TO
PRIMULAS
JODIE MITCHELL & LYNNE LAWSON

THE PLANT LOVER'S GUIDE TO
CLEMATIS
LINDA BEUTLER

THE PLANT LOVER'S GUIDE TO
MAGNOLIAS
ANDREW BUNTING